Contents

Note to the Teacher v

Timed Reading — Checking Homework — Homework Chart and
Point System — Letter to Parents — Homework Chart

Lesson	Page	Lesson	Page
Lesson 1 1		Lesson 27 53	
Lesson 2 3		Lesson 28 55	
Lesson 3 5		Lesson 29 57	
Lesson 4 7		Lesson 30 59	
Lesson 5 9		Lesson 31 61	
Lesson 6 11		Lesson 32 63	
Lesson 7 13		Lesson 33 65	
Lesson 8 15		Lesson 34 67	
Lesson 9 17		Lesson 35 69	
Lesson 10 19		Lesson 36 71	
Lesson 11 21		Lesson 37 73	
Lesson 12 23		Lesson 38 75	
Lesson 13 25		Lesson 39 77	
Lesson 14 27		Lesson 40 79	
Lesson 15 29		Lesson 41 81	
Lesson 16 31		Lesson 42 83	
Lesson 17 33		Lesson 43 85	
Lesson 18 35		Lesson 44 87	
Lesson 19 37		Lesson 45 89	
Lesson 20 39		Lesson 46 91	
Lesson 21 41		Lesson 47 93	
Lesson 22 43		Lesson 48 95	
Lesson 23 45		Lesson 49 97	
Lesson 24 47		Lesson 50 99	
Lesson 25 49		Lesson 51 101	
Lesson 26 51		Lesson 52 103	

Contents

Lesson	Page
Lesson 53	105
Lesson 54	107
Lesson 55	109
Lesson 56	111
Lesson 57	113
Lesson 58	115
Lesson 59	117

Lesson	Page
Lesson 60	119
Lesson 61	121
Lesson 62	123
Lesson 63	125
Lesson 64	127
Lesson 65	129

Answer Key ▪ Lessons 1–65 131

Corrective Reading

Enrichment Blackline Masters

Decoding B2 Decoding Strategies

Siegfried Engelmann

Gary Johnson

McGraw Hill **SRA**

Columbus, OH

SRAonline.com

 SRA

Printed in the United States of America.

Send all inquiries to this address:
SRA/McGraw-Hill
4400 Easton Commons
Columbus, OH 43219

ISBN: 978-0-07-611234-0
MHID: 0-07-611234-9

7 8 9 MAL 13 12 11 10

The *McGraw-Hill* Companies

Corrective Reading
Decoding B2
Enrichment Blackline Masters

Note to the Teacher

The activities in this book reinforce the skills taught in the 2008 edition of the *Corrective Reading Decoding B2* program. Each activity provides practice in an essential reading skill, such as

- word identification
- correct spelling of words
- spelling of words with endings such as **s, ed, ing, er, ly,** and **en**
- spelling of root words without those endings
- writing compound and other two-part words
- writing contractions
- writing sentences
- answering comprehension questions about story passages
- demonstrating comprehension of details in stories
- sequencing activities in a story
- identifying main characters
- building oral reading fluency

(Skills are identified at the bottom of each page.)

The materials are designed to be completed as study-time homework assignments. The students are not to use the Student Book when completing the Blackline Master. (The *Decoding B2* Student Book and Workbook should usually remain at school.) The Blackline Master pages correspond by lesson number to the *Decoding B2* lesson numbers. The Blackline Masters should be assigned as homework on the <u>same day</u> that the corresponding lesson is <u>completed</u> at school.

Students should be able to complete the homework assignments without any special instructions from the teacher or from a parent. On pages vii through ix are procedures for introducing the Letter to Parents and Lessons 1 through 4 Blackline Master homework assignments.

Timed Reading

To provide additional practice in building oral reading fluency, someone at home can listen to the student read aloud. These timed readings begin at Lesson 4. The procedure is similar to that of the regular program timed readings, which begin at Lesson 2. The passage which appears in the second page of the Blackline Masters for Lessons 4 through 65 is taken from the first part of the story from the previous lesson. For Lesson 4, students read part of the story from Lesson 3 at home, and so forth. The student reads aloud for 1 minute to a parent or listener who follows along and signals when the student is to stop. The number of words read in 1 minute and the number of errors are recorded, and the parent/listener signs at the bottom of the page. The student returns the signed page to school on the next school day as part of the daily two-page homework assignment.

Checking Homework

The homework should be checked each day. The most efficient procedure is to conduct a teacher-directed group workcheck. Use the annotated answer key beginning on page 131 of this book. Monitor students as they mark their own papers. Scan students' written responses for accuracy and legibility.

- For exercises that require the writing of whole words or word parts, call on individual students to spell the words as they should appear in their answers.
- For comprehension items, call on individual students to read each question and say the correct answer.

- For activities in which students fill in the missing words in a passage, call on individual students to read the passage aloud and say the word that should appear in the blank.
- If the group is large, read the correct answers for each item as students check their own papers.

Homework Chart and Point System

Keep a record of the completed homework assignments. A reproducible Homework Chart appears on page xi. Or you may elect to have students record points in the Point Chart in their Workbook. Points earned can be recorded in the Bonus box for the regular lesson.

Points could be awarded as follows:

completing homework	2 points
0 errors	2 points
1 or 2 errors	1 point
more than 2 errors	0 points

When the timed readings begin at Lesson 4:

completing the homework reading checkout	2 points

If you award points for homework assignments, you will need to modify the number of points required in the regular program to earn various letter grades. (For a discussion of points and letter grades, see "The Management System" section in the *Decoding B2 Teacher's Guide*.) An alternative procedure would be to make the points earned for homework assignments separate from those earned in the regular program and to provide special incentives for completing homework.

The Blackline Master homework pages are designed so that students can be successful. Once students learn that they can complete homework successfully, they will be motivated to continue to do so. If the teacher provides positive verbal feedback about completing homework assignments, along with the use of points, students will be encouraged to do well, and their reading performance will continue to improve.

Letter to Parents

A letter explaining the general procedures for homework assignments appears on page x. This letter should be sent home along with the first homework assignment.

Dear Parents,

Students are expected to complete homework as part of their reading lessons. The homework activities provide practice in essential reading skills. In the daily homework exercises, students receive practice in the following reading skills:

- identifying words
- spelling words with endings and words without endings
- writing sentences
- answering questions about story passages
- building oral reading fluency

The homework consists of two pages. Starting at Lesson 4, on the second page is a story passage that the student is to read aloud to someone at home. This activity provides practice on speed and accuracy.

You will need a digital watch, a digital timer (such as a kitchen timer), or a clock with a sweep second hand so that you can time the student for exactly 1 minute. The student starts at the first word of the passage and reads for 1 minute. You keep track of the mistakes the student makes. The goal is for the student to read exactly what is on the page.

Here are the kinds of errors to count:

- saying the wrong word or mispronouncing a word
- adding a word
- leaving out a word
- adding an ending to a word (for example, reading "plays" for play)
- leaving off an ending (for example, reading "start" for started)
- not stopping at the end of a sentence
- rereading part of a sentence

At the end of 1 minute, stop the student. Write the number of words read in 1 minute and the number of errors in the blanks at the bottom of the page.

If the student wants to read the passage again, write the number of times the passage was read in the blank at the bottom of the page.

Sign at the bottom of the page. The student should return the two-page homework assignment to school on the next school day.

Remember to be patient. Students who try hard need to know that they are improving. Your assistance each day will help the student improve. The more practice the student receives, the faster the student will become a better reader.

Thank you.

Introducing the Letter to Parents and Lesson 1 Homework

Note: Students are not to use the Student Book or Workbook when completing the Blackline Master homework assignments.

Here are procedures for introducing the Letter to Parents and Lesson 1 homework.

1. Pass out the Letter to Parents.

Take this letter home. After you complete your homework, have it signed. Bring the homework back to school (tomorrow). Starting at Lesson 4, you will do timed readings at home, too.

2. Pass out the homework for Lesson 1. Touch the instructions for Part 1. ✓

I'll read the instructions: "Write these words without endings." This exercise is like the one you did in your Workbook.

Some of the words will have a final **E.** Other words won't. Remember, if the letter just before the underlined part is a vowel, you write the word with a final **E.** If the letter just before the underlined part is a consonant, you write the word without a final **E.**

3. Touch Part 2. ✓

I'll read the instructions: "Read the words in the box. Then fill in the blanks." You'll use words from the box to fill in the blanks so that the passage makes sense.

4. Touch Part 3. ✓

I'll read the instructions: "Copy the sentences." You will copy the sentences on the lines.

5. Touch Part 4. ✓

I'll read the instructions: "Write these words with **E-D** endings." All the words will have **E-D** endings.

6. Touch Part 5. ✓

I'll read the instructions: "Read the sentences in the box. Then write the answer to each question." The questions are below the box.

7. Touch Part 6. ✓

I'll read the instructions: "Match the words and complete them." This exercise is like the one you did in your Workbook.

8. Remember to have your homework signed at home and bring it to school (tomorrow).

Lesson 1

Name _____

Part 1
Write these words without endings.

1. stri<u>pes</u> _____   5. cho<u>ked</u> _____
2. stin<u>ker</u> _____   6. blus<u>hed</u> _____
3. no<u>ses</u> _____   7. clo<u>ser</u> _____
4. smal<u>ler</u> _____   8. tal<u>ked</u> _____

Part 2
Read the words in the box. Then fill in the blanks.

horse	ten	garden	six	tips	striped
see	five	mad	stripes	smell	stand
stinker	brown	hear	proud	middle	look

There were _____ stink bugs that lived in a _____. Stink bugs are proud if they can make a big stink. The biggest stink bug was very _____. She said, "This is how to make a stink." And she made a big stink that you could _____ on the other side of the garden.

One stink bug had a _____ back. He said, "If a bug has stripes on its back, it has the best _____. Here I go."

Part 3
Copy the sentences.
A bird was flying over the garden.

_____

The smallest bug had stripes on its back.

_____

We are in the middle of a contest.

_____

Suffixes, vocabulary/context clues, copying sentences

Copyright © SRA/McGraw-Hill. Permission is granted to reproduce for classroom use.   Lesson 1   1

Lesson 1

Name _____

Part 4
Write these words with ed endings.

1. jump _____   4. talk _____
2. fish _____   5. smell _____
3. form _____   6. trick _____

Part 5
Read the sentences in the box. Then write the answer to each question.

> The little bug kept talking. She said, "One time, I made a stink that was so powerful it turned all the grass brown. I'll bet that I can beat ten skunks in a stinking contest."

1. What happened when the little bug made a powerful stink? _____

2. What did the little bug bet? _____

Part 6
Match the words and complete them.

snow	•	•	chomp
chomping	•	•	sing
sings	•	•	er
night	•	•	ow
summer	•	•	n

| A Note to the Parent | Work was completed at home. |

(Parent's/Listener's) signature _____ Date _____

Suffixes, inferences, word completion

2   Lesson 1   Copyright © SRA/McGraw-Hill. Permission is granted to reproduce for classroom use.

Introducing Lesson 2 Homework

Here are procedures for introducing Lesson 2 homework.

1. Pass out the homework.

Touch the instructions for Part 1. ✓

I'll read the instructions: "Write these words without endings." This exercise is like the one you did in your Workbook. Some of the words will have a final **E.** Other words won't. Remember to look at the letter just before the underlined part.

2. Touch Part 2. ✓

I'll read the instructions: "Match the words and complete them." This exercise is like the one you did in your workbook.

3. Touch Part 3. ✓

You'll read the sentences in the box and answer the questions.

4. Touch Part 4. ✓

You'll use words from the box to fill in the blanks so that the passage makes sense.

5. Touch Part 5. ✓

I'll read the instructions: "Write these words with **E-R** endings." All the words will have **E-R** endings.

6. Touch Part 6. ✓

You'll copy the sentences on the lines.

7. Remember to have your homework signed at home and bring it to school (tomorrow).

Introducing Lesson 3 Homework

Remind students to complete the work at home, have it signed, and return it the next day.

Lesson 2

Name _____

Part 1
Write these words without endings.

1. talking _____   5. shopped _____
2. taking _____   6. stinker _____
3. striped _____   7. closed _____
4. bigger _____   8. packed _____

Part 2
Match the words and complete them.

_____ forest •   • and _____
_____ began •   • si _____
_____ stand •   • gl _____
_____ sick •   • est _____
_____ glad •   • be _____

Part 3
Read the sentences in the box. Then write the answer to each question.

> The little bug asked, "Are you grabbing on to something? Nobody can stand up when my stink reaches them. First it hits them so hard that they fall down. Then it knocks the air from them. And when it has done that, my stink chokes them up. But most bugs don't die from the smell. They are just sick for weeks."

1. What is the first thing that happens to other bugs when they smell the little bug's stink?

_____

2. How long are the bugs sick from the stink? _____

Suffixes, word completion, inferences

Copyright © SRA/McGraw-Hill. Permission is granted to reproduce for classroom use.   Lesson 2   3

Lesson 2

Name _____

Part 4
Read the words in the box. Then fill in the blanks.

trying	fort	cloud	best	telling	leave
fainting	contest	smallest	stand	shown	told
left	blush	garden	whiff	taking	laughing

There was a _____ in the _____ Five stink bugs were _____ to see who had the _____ stinker. All of the bugs but one had _____ off their best stink. Now that bug began telling the others how good she was at _____ She talked and talked about the _____. Soon only the biggest bug was _____

Part 5
Write these words with er endings.

1. cold _____   5. deep _____
2. stick _____   6. fast _____
3. hard _____   7. help _____
4. talk _____   8. stink _____

Part 6
Copy the sentences.
Breathe in deeply and hold in the air.

_____

She went to the other side of the garden.

_____

> **A Note to the Parent**   Work was completed at home.
> (Parent's/Listener's) signature _____ Date _____

Vocabulary/context clues; inflectional suffixes, sentence copying

4   Lesson 2   Copyright © SRA/McGraw-Hill. Permission is granted to reproduce for classroom use.

Introducing Lessons 4–65 Homework

Tell students that starting with Lesson 4 and continuing through Lesson 65, they will complete a timed reading at home as part of the homework assignment. The procedures are the same as when they do a timed reading with their checkout partner at school. The Letter to Parents explains the procedures in detail.

Lesson 4   Name _____

Part 1
Write these words with ed endings.

1. coach _____
2. blush _____
3. toss _____

Part 2
Write these words with es endings.

1. coach _____
2. blush _____
3. toss _____

Part 3
Write the two words that make up each word.

1. herself = _____ + _____
2. basketball = _____ + _____
3. sometimes = _____ + _____
4. motorboat = _____ + _____
5. everyone = _____ + _____
6. anything = _____ + _____

Part 4
Write these words without endings.

1. rais<u>ing</u> _____
2. grab<u>bed</u> _____
3. smil<u>ed</u> _____
4. near<u>ly</u> _____
5. sai<u>led</u> _____
6. deep<u>ly</u> _____
7. skip<u>ping</u> _____
8. ro<u>ses</u> _____

Vocabulary/suffixes, compound words

Lesson 4   7

Lesson 4   Name _____

Part 5

Lonely Art

Art was a farm boy. He talked like a farm boy. He walked	13
like a farm boy. And when he was thirteen years old, he began	26
to grow. When he was fifteen years old, he was taller than any	39
other kid. His arms seemed too long. He looked like a long	51
blade of grass.	54
After school, he didn't hang out with the other kids in his	66
class. He went home to work on the farm. The other kids in his	80
class said, "Art's a loner. He never hangs out with us." They	92
didn't know that Art was shy.	98
A teacher in the school told Art that he should go out	110
for basketball. And Art did. But he hadn't played basketball	120
before. And he wasn't any good. He couldn't shoot the ball. He	132
couldn't block shots. He couldn't dribble the ball.	140
The coach said, "Art, this game is too hard for you. Why	152
don't you try out for another sport?"	159
But Art didn't try another sport. After school, he went	169
down to the pond near his farm house. He skipped stones on	181
the pond. He said to himself, "I just wish there were a	193
stone-skipping team. I'd be the champ of that team."	202

 A Note to the Parent   Listen to the student read the passage. Count the number of words read in one minute and the number of errors.

Number of words read _____   Number of errors _____

We read the story _____ times.

(Parent's/Listener's) signature _____

Date _____

Reading fluency

8   Lesson 4

Dear Parents,

Students are expected to complete homework as part of their reading lessons. The homework activities provide practice in essential reading skills. In the daily homework exercises, students receive practice in the following reading skills:

- identifying words
- spelling words with endings and words without endings
- writing sentences
- answering questions about story passages
- building oral reading fluency

The homework consists of two pages. Starting at Lesson 4, on the second page is a story passage that the student is to read aloud to someone at home. This activity provides practice on speed and accuracy.

You will need a digital watch, a digital timer (such as a kitchen timer), or a clock with a sweep second hand so that you can time the student for exactly 1 minute. The student starts at the first word of the passage and reads for 1 minute. You keep track of the mistakes the student makes. The goal is for the student to read exactly what is on the page.

Here are the kinds of errors to count:

- saying the wrong word or mispronouncing a word
- adding a word
- leaving out a word
- adding an ending to a word (for example, reading "plays" for *play*)
- leaving off an ending (for example, reading "start" for *started*)
- not stopping at the end of a sentence
- rereading part of a sentence

At the end of 1 minute, stop the student. Write the number of words read in 1 minute and the number of errors in the blanks at the bottom of the page.

If the student wants to read the passage again, write the number of times the passage was read in the blank at the bottom of the page.

Sign at the bottom of the page. The student should return the two-page homework assignment to school on the next school day.

Remember to be patient. Students who try hard need to know that they are improving. Your assistance each day will help the student improve. The more practice the student receives, the faster the student will become a better reader.

Thank you.

Corrective Reading   Decoding B2 Homework Chart

Teacher _____   Group _____

Student	Date	Lesson Number																												

Lesson 1

Name _____

Part 1

Write these words without endings.

1. str<u>ipes</u> _____

2. stink<u>er</u> _____

3. n<u>oses</u> _____

4. sma<u>ller</u> _____

5. cho<u>ked</u> _____

6. blus<u>hed</u> _____

7. clo<u>ser</u> _____

8. tal<u>ked</u> _____

Part 2

Read the words in the box. Then fill in the blanks.

horse	ten	garden	six	tips	striped
see	five	mad	stripes	smell	stand
stinker	brown	hear	proud	middle	look

There were _____ stink bugs that lived in a _____. Stink bugs are proud if they can make a big stink. The biggest stink bug was very _____. She said, "This is how to make a stink." And she made a big stink that you could _____ on the other side of the garden.

One stink bug had a _____ back. He said, "If a bug has stripes on its back, it has the best _____. Here I go."

Part 3

Copy the sentences.

A bird was flying over the garden.

_____

The smallest bug had stripes on its back.

_____

We are in the middle of a contest.

_____

Suffixes, vocabulary/context clues, copying sentences

Part 4

Write these words with **ed** endings.

1. jump _____   4. talk _____

2. fish _____   5. smell _____

3. form _____   6. trick _____

Part 5

Read the sentences in the box. Then write the answer to each question.

> The little bug kept talking. She said, "One time, I made a stink that was so powerful it turned all the grass brown. I'll bet that I can beat ten skunks in a stinking contest."

1. What happened when the little bug made a powerful stink? _____

_____

2. What did the little bug bet? _____

_____

Part 6

Match the words and complete them.

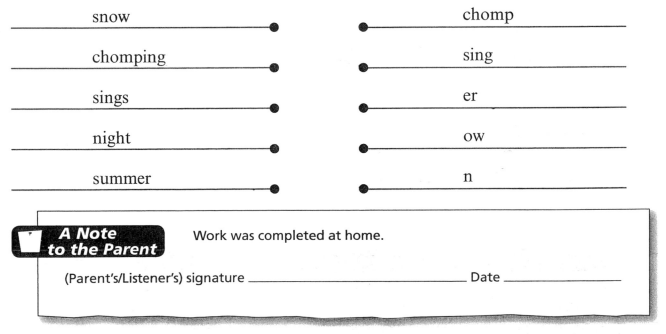

_____ snow   ●   ●   chomp _____

_____ chomping   ●   ●   sing _____

_____ sings   ●   ●   er _____

_____ night   ●   ●   ow _____

_____ summer   ●   ●   n _____

A Note to the Parent   Work was completed at home.

(Parent's/Listener's) signature _____ Date _____

Suffixes, inferences, word completion

Name _____

Part 1

Write these words without endings.

1. talking _____

2. taking _____

3. striped _____

4. bigger _____

5. shopped _____

6. stinker _____

7. closed _____

8. packed _____

Part 2

Match the words and complete them.

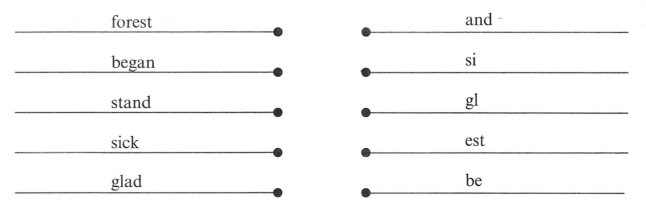

_____ forest •   • and

_____ began •   • si

_____ stand •   • gl

_____ sick •   • est

_____ glad •   • be

Part 3

Read the sentences in the box. Then write the answer to each question.

> The little bug asked, "Are you grabbing on to something? Nobody can stand up when my stink reaches them. First it hits them so hard that they fall down. Then it knocks the air from them. And when it has done that, my stink chokes them up. But most bugs don't die from the smell. They are just sick for weeks."

1. What is the first thing that happens to other bugs when they smell the little bug's stink?

_____

2. How long are the bugs sick from the stink? _____

Suffixes, word completion, inferences

Name _____

Part 4

Read the words in the box. Then fill in the blanks.

trying	fort	cloud	best	telling	leave
fainting	contest	smallest	stand	shown	told
left	blush	garden	whiff	taking	stinking

There was a _____ in the _____. Five stink bugs were _____ to see

who had the _____ stinker. All of the bugs but one had _____ off their best

stink. Now that bug began telling the others how good she was at _____. She talked and

talked. The other bugs began to _____. Soon only the biggest bug was _____.

Part 5

Write these words with **er** endings.

1. cold _____

2. stick _____

3. hard _____

4. talk _____

5. deep _____

6. fast _____

7. help _____

8. stink _____

Part 6

Copy the sentences.

Breathe in deeply and hold in the air.

_____

She went to the other side of the garden.

_____

> **A Note to the Parent**
>
> Work was completed at home.
>
> (Parent's/Listener's) signature _____ Date _____

Vocabulary/context clues; inflectional suffixes, sentence copying

Lesson 3

Name _____

Part 1
Write these words without endings.

1. as<u>ked</u>   _____

2. lo<u>ner</u>   _____

3. win<u>ked</u>   _____

4. skip<u>ped</u>   _____

5. ma<u>king</u>   _____

6. plan<u>ned</u>   _____

7. wal<u>ked</u>   _____

8. clo<u>ser</u>   _____

Part 2
Follow the instructions for each item.

1. Write the word **couch.** Make a line under **ou.**   _____

2. Write the word **coach.** Make a line over **oa.**   _____

3. Write the word **pail.** Make a line over **ai.**   _____

Part 3
Write these words with er endings.

1. tell   _____

2. farm   _____

3. teach   _____

4. old   _____

Part 4
Write these words with ing endings.

1. wait   _____

2. laugh   _____

3. look   _____

4. walk   _____

Suffixes, sound/symbol correspondence

Part 5

Match the words and complete them.

pond _____ •	• _____ teen
grow _____ •	• _____ gr
thirteen _____ •	• _____ po
block _____ •	• _____ ied
tried _____ •	• _____ ock

Part 6

Read the sentences in the box. Then write the answer to each question.

> After school, Art didn't hang out with the other kids in his class. He went home to work on the farm. The other kids in his class said, "Art's a loner. He never hangs out with us." They didn't know that Art was shy.

1. What did Art do after school? _____

2. Why did the other kids say, "Art is a loner"? _____

_____

Part 7

Copy the sentences.

He skipped stones on the pond.

_____

She went to class on time.

_____

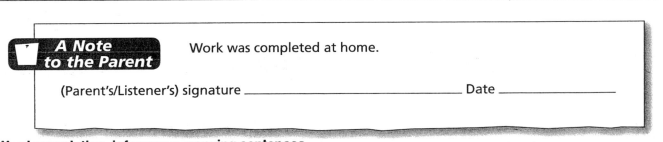

A Note to the Parent   Work was completed at home.

(Parent's/Listener's) signature _____ Date _____

Word completion, inferences, copying sentences

Name _____

Part 1

Write these words with **ed** endings.

1. coach   _____

2. blush   _____

3. toss   _____

Part 2

Write these words with **es** endings.

1. coach   _____

2. blush   _____

3. toss   _____

Part 3

Write the two words that make up each word.

1. herself   =   _____ + _____

2. basketball   =   _____ + _____

3. sometimes   =   _____ + _____

4. motorboat   =   _____ + _____

5. everyone   =   _____ + _____

6. anything   =   _____ + _____

Part 4

Write these words without endings.

1. raising   _____

2. grabbed   _____

3. smiled   _____

4. nearly   _____

5. sailed   _____

6. deeply   _____

7. skipping   _____

8. roses   _____

Vocabulary/suffixes, compound words

Part 5

Lonely Art

Art was a farm boy. He talked like a farm boy. He walked	13
like a farm boy. And when he was thirteen years old, he began	26
to grow. When he was fifteen years old, he was taller than any	39
other kid. His arms seemed too long. He looked like a long	51
blade of grass.	54
After school, he didn't hang out with the other kids in his	66
class. He went home to work on the farm. The other kids in his	80
class said, "Art's a loner. He never hangs out with us." They	92
didn't know that Art was shy.	98
A teacher in the school told Art that he should go out	110
for basketball. And Art did. But he hadn't played basketball	120
before. And he wasn't any good. He couldn't shoot the ball. He	132
couldn't block shots. He couldn't dribble the ball.	140
The coach said, "Art, this game is too hard for you. Why	152
don't you try out for another sport?"	159
But Art didn't try another sport. After school, he went	169
down to the pond near his farm house. He skipped stones on	181
the pond. He said to himself, "I just wish there were a	193
stone-skipping team. I'd be the champ of that team."	202

A Note to the Parent

Listen to the student read the passage. Count the number of words read in one minute and the number of errors.

Number of words read _____ Number of errors _____

We read the story _____ times.

(Parent's/Listener's) signature _____

Date _____

Reading fluency

Name _____

Part 1

Write these words with **er** endings.

1. play _____

2. small _____

3. catch _____

4. long _____

Part 2

Write these words with **ed endings.**

1. lean _____

2. walk _____

3. yell _____

4. dress _____

Part 3

Write the two words that make up each word.

1. baseball = _____ + _____

2. someone = _____ + _____

Part 4

Write **1, 2,** or **3** in front of each sentence to show when these things happened in the story. Then write the sentences in the blanks.

_____ Art didn't sleep well that night.

_____ Art tossed pitches to the catcher.

_____ The coach said, "Art, I would like you to come out for baseball.

1. _____

_____

2. _____

_____

3. _____

_____

Suffixes, compound words, sequence

Name _____

Part 5

The Baseball Lot

Art was having a bad time in school. The kids didn't talk	12
with him, and he didn't know what to say to them. After	24
school, Art would go to the pond to skip stones. And as he	37
skipped them, he said the things he would like to say to Patty.	50
"Patty," he said to himself one day, "I want you to be my	63
girl friend." He skipped a stone and looked at it as it sailed	76
almost to the other side of the pond. Then he said, "No, I will	90
never say anything like that to Patty. I would just blush, and I	103
wouldn't be able to say anything."	109
After school one day, Art saw Patty standing on the corner	120
near school. He walked up to her. "Hi, Art," she said.	131
"Hi," he said. He breathed in deeply and said, "Can I walk	143
with you?"	145
She smiled and said, "I'm waiting for somebody, Art.	154
Sorry."	155
"That's okay," Art said, and he began to walk down the	166
street. He looked back from time to time. When he was about a	179
block away, he saw Mark Jackson walk up to Patty and begin to	192
walk with her.	195
The next day, one of the kids told him that Mark Jackson	207
was Patty's boy friend.	211

A Note to the Parent

Listen to the student read the passage. Count the number of words read in one minute and the number of errors.

Number of words read _____   Number of errors _____

We read the story _____ times.

(Parent's/Listener's) signature _____

Date _____

Reading fluency

Lesson 6

Name _____

Part 1

Write these words without endings.

1. whipped _____

2. laughing _____

3. leaned _____

4. tallest _____

5. raises _____

6. blushed _____

7. stones _____

8. faking _____

Part 2

Match the words and complete them.

started _____●   ●_____ eep

springing _____●   ●_____ sm

deeply _____●   ●_____ ar

smiled _____●   ●_____ ing

closer _____●   ●_____ cl

Part 3

Write **1, 2,** or **3** in front of each sentence to show when these things happened in the story. Then write the sentences in the blanks.

_____ Art kept telling himself what he should not do.

_____ Art didn't sleep well before the game with West High.

_____ He leaned back and tossed the ball about nine feet over the catcher's mitt.

1. _____

_____

2. _____

_____

3. _____

_____

Suffixes, word completion, sequence

Part 4

Art's Fast Ball

Art didn't know what to do. He wanted to leave, but	11
everybody was yelling, "Come on, Art, show us how to pitch."	22
Some boys grabbed Art and started to lead him to the	33
pitcher's mound. "Here he is, Coach," one of the boys hollered.	44
"The star pitcher."	47
The coach walked up to Art. He said, "I don't know what	59
this is all about, but we've got work to do out here. So throw	73
the ball to the catcher. That will shut those guys up. Then get	86
out of here."	89
"Okay," Art said. The coach handed him the ball.	98
Art turned to the coach and said, "Do I just try to throw it	112
at the catcher as hard as I can?"	120
"That's right," the coach said. "Just throw it and get out of	132
here."	133
The ball felt a little too big in Art's hand. It didn't seem to	147
fit as well as a skipping stone. He rubbed it a few times and got	162
a good grip on it. Then he leaned back.	171
"Show them how—if you can," the boys yelled.	180
Art's long arm went back like a whip. Then it came forward	192
like a whip. "Zip—pow." The catcher was on his seat.	203

A Note to the Parent Listen to the student read the passage. Count the number of words read in one minute and the number of errors.

Number of words read _____ Number of errors _____

We read the story _____ times.

(Parent's/Listener's) signature _____

Date _____

Reading fluency

Lesson 7

Name _____

Part 1

Read the sentences and answer the questions.

Art remembered that Bob was the best batter on the West team.

For a moment, Art began to think about the things that he should not do.

1. Who was Bob? _____

2. When Art remembered about Bob, what did Art begin to think about? _____

_____

3. For how long did Art think about those things? _____

Part 2

Write these words without endings.

1. deeply   _____   **5.** baker   _____

2. grabbed   _____   **6.** taking   _____

3. loudly   _____   **7.** smiling   _____

4. smartest   _____   **8.** muttered   _____

Part 3

Read the words in the box. Then fill in the blanks.

stared	start	up	hugged	sat	passed
hit	leaned	cheered	pitch	swing	shake
jumped	throw	down	reached	clapped	tossed

Art _____ back and—"Zip—pow." The catcher was _____. And the

batter began to _____ after the ball had _____ the catcher.

    The fans from Art's school cheered and cheered. They _____ up and down. They

_____ each other. They yelled, "Go to it, Art. Show them how to pitch."

Details, suffixes, vocabulary/context clues

Lesson 7   **13**

Part 4

The School Team

The coach wanted Art to show him everything he could do	11
with a baseball. The catcher had stuffed a rag into his mitt so	24
that Art's fast ball would not sting his hand so much.	35
"Let's see your fast ball," the coach said.	43
Art leaned back and—"Zip—pow." The catcher said, "Ow!	53
That rag doesn't help very much." He tossed the ball back to	65
Art.	66
Art dropped the ball. He picked it up and looked at the	78
coach. The coach said, "Now can you make the ball curve?"	89
"What do you mean?" Art asked.	95
"Make the ball bend to the left or bend to the right."	107
"Oh, that," Art said. "Which way do you want me to make	119
it bend?"	121
The coach stared at Art for a moment. Then he said, "Make	133
it curve to the left."	138
"Okay," Art said.	141
Art leaned back and to the side. He said to himself, "This is	154
just like making a stone curve to the left."	163
Art's arm whipped out to the side, and the ball went flying.	175
It was going far to the right of the catcher. The catcher began to	189
reach to the right. Then the ball curved and hit him in the chest.	203

A Note to the Parent

Listen to the student read the passage. Count the number of words read in one minute and the number of errors.

Number of words read _____   Number of errors _____

We read the story _____ times.

(Parent's/Listener's) signature _____

Date _____

Reading fluency

Name _____

Part 1

Read the sentences in the box. Then write the answer to each question.

> After the first game, things were different in school. The kids smiled at Art. They went out of their way to talk to him. Art felt a lot better about school. In fact, school was a lot of fun for Art now. He waved to the girls. He wasn't afraid to talk to girls. He didn't look down when he talked to them. He had done that before, but now he was Art the Star, the big pitcher.

1. When were things different in school for Art? _____

2. Name two ways that things were different in school. _____

_____

3. Why wasn't Art afraid to talk to the girls now? _____

_____

Part 2

Write these words without endings.

1. rider　　　_____

2. riding　　　_____

3. smiles　　　_____

4. remembered　　　_____

5. groaned　　　_____

6. patted　　　_____

Part 3

Read the sentences and answer the questions.

Art said to Patty, "If that's the way you want it," and walked down the hall.

He started to whistle, just to show her that he didn't care if she went with him.

1. Who walked down the hall? _____

2. Why did Art start whistling? _____

_____

3. What did Art do as he walked down the hall? _____

Make inferences, suffixes, draw conclusions based on evidence

Part 4

Some Bad Pitches

Art had just thrown a bad ball. And the West High fans were	13
cheering and clapping. "That's the way to pitch," they yelled.	23
The catcher tossed the ball back to Art, and Art dropped it.	35
The West High fans cheered again. The fans from Art's school	46
were silent.	48
Art picked up the ball. He breathed in and out three times.	60
Then he said to himself, "Don't throw the ball too high. Don't	72
throw the ball too high." Art was not thinking well again.	83
Art heaved the ball. It went like a streak. But it went about	96
ten feet over the catcher's head. The catcher called time out and	108
ran to the pitcher's mound.	113
The fans from West High cheered. "Get another pitcher,"	122
they yelled. "This one has had it."	129
The catcher said, "What's the matter, Art?"	136
"I don't know," Art said. His hand was shaking. "I can't	147
make the ball go where I want it to go."	157
"Yes, you can, Art," the catcher said. "Just think about skipping	168
stones. I'll hold out my mitt. You must throw that ball right into the	182
mitt. Throw it just like you throw a stone. You can do it."	195
"I'll try," Art said.	199
The catcher jogged back, and Art rubbed the ball around in	210
his hand.	212

A Note to the Parent

Listen to the student read the passage. Count the number of words read in one minute and the number of errors.

Number of words read _____   Number of errors _____

We read the story _____ times.

(Parent's/Listener's) signature _____

Date _____

Reading fluency

Name _____

Part 1
Follow the instructions for each item.

1. Write the word **would.** Make a line over **oul.**   _____

2. Write the word **almost.** Make a line over **al.**   _____

3. Write the word **ducked.** Make a line under **ck.**   _____

Part 2
Write these words with **ed endings.**

1. play   _____

2. whistle   _____

3. jog   _____

Part 3
Write these words with **er endings.**

1. bat   _____

2. start   _____

3. play   _____

Part 4
Read the sentences in the box. Then write the answer to each question.

> Before the game, some fans didn't cheer. One of the fans said, "We didn't come here to see kids play. We came to see the Reds and the Tigers."
>
> Art walked to the mound. Then he looked up at the stands. He had never seen so many fans before. Suddenly he became afraid. He began to think about all of the things that he shouldn't do. "Don't throw the ball too high," he told himself.

1. Why didn't some fans cheer? _____

_____

2. When Art looked up at the stands, what did he see? _____

_____

3. What did Art say to himself? _____

_____

Sound/symbol correspondence, suffixes, details

Part 5

Art Becomes a Star

The best batter on the West team was at the plate. Art was	13
thinking about what the catcher had told him. Art reared back.	24
He let the ball fly. "Zip—pow." The catcher was on his seat again.	38
"Strike one," the umpire called.	43
"You can do it, Bob," the West fans yelled.	52
Art got the ball again. He looked at the catcher's mitt. He	64
reared back and let the ball fly. The ball started to go right at	78
the batter. The batter ducked down. But almost before he could	89
move, the ball curved and went right into the catcher's mitt.	100
"Strike two," the umpire called.	105
Again Art wound up and let the ball fly. Bob took a big	118
swing at it, but the ball was in the catcher's mitt before Bob	131
began to swing.	134
"Strike three. You're out."	138
"Oh, no," the West High School fans groaned.	146
"Go, Art, go," the fans from Art's school yelled.	155
And Art went. He struck out every other batter in the game.	167
Art did not do well when he tried to bat, but his team was the	182
winner. They beat West High School 3 to 1.	191
Everybody from Art's school yelled and crowded around	199
Art.	200

A Note to the Parent

Listen to the student read the passage. Count the number of words read in one minute and the number of errors.

Number of words read _____ Number of errors _____

We read the story _____ times.

(Parent's/Listener's) signature _____

Date _____

Reading fluency

Name _____

Part 1

Read the sentences in the box. Then write the answer to each question.

> People from the big league came over to talk to Art that night. A man from the Reds said that he would pay Art three hundred thousand dollars if Art left school and became a pitcher for the Reds. A woman from the Tigers told Art that she would give Art five hundred thousand dollars if Art played with the Tigers.
>
> Art told them that he would have to think about leaving school.
>
> Then some of Art's friends came over. They wanted to take Art to a party. Art asked his dad and mom, and they said that it was all right for him to go.

1. How much money were the Tigers offering to give to Art if he came and pitched for them?

_____

2. Why did Art want to take time to think about the offers from the two baseball teams?

_____

_____

3. Who told Art it was okay to go to the party?

_____

Part 2

Write the name of the person or the people each sentence tells about.

Art	Art's mom and dad	Art's friends
Woman from the Tigers		**Man from the Reds**

1. These people asked Art to go to a party with them. _____

2. This person offered Art $300,000 to play baseball. _____

3. This person asked to go to a party. _____

4. This person offered Art $500,000 to play baseball. _____

5. These people said Art could go to a party. _____

Draw conclusions based on evidence, skim and scan for information/character identification

Part 3

First Inning

Art was going to pitch to some big league players before	11
the game on Sunday. His coach had told him that he would be	24
pitching to some of the best batters in baseball.	33
The game was to start at one o'clock. Art was to begin	45
pitching at noon. But at 12 o'clock there were not very many	57
fans in the stands. Art walked to the pitcher's mound and	68
picked up the ball. One of the players from the Tigers said,	80
"Just throw fast balls. The batter will hit them into the left	92
stands. Some of the fans will get free baseballs."	101
Art looked up at the left stands. About one hundred kids	112
were up there. Some of them had baseball mitts. Art said,	123
"Should I throw as hard as I can?"	131
"That's right," the player said. "Don't worry, the batter will	141
hit the ball. You're pitching to James Hunt. He'll hit them, all	153
right."	154
Art stared at the catcher's mitt. Then Art reared back and	165
gave the ball the hardest heave he could give it. "Zip—pow."	177
The catcher was on his seat.	183
The player who was standing next to Art blinked and stared at	195
Art. James Hunt looked at the catcher, and then he looked at Art.	208

A Note to the Parent

Listen to the student read the passage. Count the number of words read in one minute and the number of errors.

Number of words read _____   Number of errors _____

We read the story _____ times.

(Parent's/Listener's) signature _____

Date _____

Reading fluency

Name _____

Part 1

Write these words without endings.

1. nearly _____   5. falling _____

2. speaker _____   6. mixed _____

3. leaving _____   7. skipped _____

4. winner _____   8. smallest _____

Part 2

Match the words and complete them.

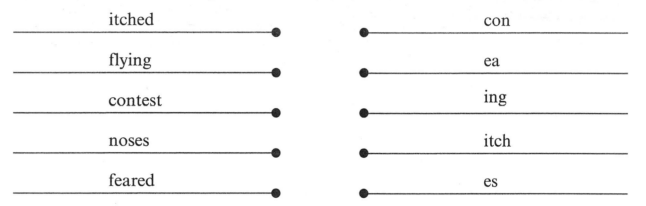

_____ itched ●   ● con _____

_____ flying ●   ● ea _____

_____ contest ●   ● ing _____

_____ noses ●   ● itch _____

_____ feared ●   ● es _____

Part 3

Write the two words that make up each word.

1. handshake = _____ + _____

2. basketball = _____ + _____

3. somewhere = _____ + _____

4. spotlight = _____ + _____

Suffixes, compound words, word completion

Name _____

Part 4

Things Take a Bad Turn

Art was standing on the pitcher's mound. His hands felt	10
cold. The fans were yelling and booing because he had dropped	21
the ball. The catcher yelled to him, "Come on, Art. Just zip it	34
right in here." He pounded his fist into his mitt.	44
Art stared at that mitt. He stared and stared. "Look at	55
that mitt," he told himself. Now he was thinking the right way	67
again. He said, "I'm going to zip that ball right into the mitt."	80
He leaned back and shot the ball at the catcher's mitt. The	92
batter didn't have time to start his swing. The catcher was on	104
his seat.	106
"Strike one," the umpire called.	111
The fans began to say, "Did you see that?" Then the fans	123
fell silent as Art reared back for his next pitch. "Zip—pow."	135
Down went the catcher again.	140
"Strike two."	142
"Wow!" the fans yelled. Then they waited for Art's next pitch.	153
Again Art heaved the ball so hard that the batter did not	165
have time to swing. "Strike three. You're out."	173
The fans clapped and cheered.	178
Art struck out the next batter with three pitches.	187
The last batter took a swing at Art's fast ball, but he missed	200
it by a foot.	204

A Note to the Parent

Listen to the student read the passage. Count the number of words read in one minute and the number of errors.

Number of words read _____ Number of errors _____

We read the story _____ times.

(Parent's/Listener's) signature _____

Date _____

Reading fluency

Part 1

Read the sentences in the box. Then write the answer to each question.

> Art didn't talk to Patty for a month. He moped around school, and he moped around the farm. He went to the doctor's office three times a week. The doctor had him do exercises for his arm.
>
> Now Art could bend his arm almost all the way. But his arm was weak. It was so weak that he couldn't bend it when he held a heavy steel ball. The doctor told him that he should exercise his arm at home every day, but Art didn't feel like exercising. So his arm didn't get very strong.

1. Art moped around school and around the farm. What does **mope** mean? _____

_____

2. What did the doctor tell Art that he should do? _____

_____

3. Why didn't Art's arm get very strong? _____

_____

Part 2

Write these words with **ed** endings.

1. sail _____

2. clap _____

3. lean _____

4. pass _____

5. scratch _____

Part 3

Write these words with **ing** endings.

1. yell _____

2. think _____

3. sit _____

4. dream _____

5. drive _____

Draw conclusions based on evidence, suffixes

Name _____

Part 4

He'll Never Pitch Again

Art was in the hospital. The nurse had just told him that he	13
had been in a very bad crash. Art didn't remember the crash.	25
He had a hard time thinking. His arm was in pain.	36
A doctor came into the room. The nurse said, "He's awake	47
now."	48
The doctor walked up to Art's bed. "How do you feel?" she	60
asked.	61
"I don't know," Art said. It was hard to think. "There's a	73
pain in my right arm. Why is it in a cast?"	84
"Your arm is broken," the doctor said.	91
"That's the arm I throw with," Art said. "Is it bad? Will I be	105
able to pitch soon?"	109
The doctor looked down. Then she stood up. "We should	119
talk about this later," she said. "Right now, you should get some	131
sleep."	132
"Tell me," Art said. "Will my arm be okay?"	141
The doctor rubbed her chin. "I'm afraid not," she said.	151
"Your arm was broken in three spots. I don't think you'll ever	163
be able to pitch again."	168
"No," Art said. "No, no." He began to sob. Art wanted to	180
curl up into a little ball and hide. He wanted to be somewhere	193
else. He wanted to believe that he was having a bad dream.	205

A Note to the Parent Listen to the student read the passage. Count the number of words read in one minute and the number of errors.

Number of words read _____ Number of errors _____

We read the story _____ times.

(Parent's/Listener's) signature _____

Date _____

Reading fluency

Part 1

Write the words.

out + side = _____

any + where = _____

your + self = _____

cheer + leader = _____

Part 2

Read the sentences in the box. Then write the answer to each question.

> Art said, "I once read that a bird with a broken wing never flies as high again."
> Patty said, "Stop that. You're not a bird, and you don't have a broken wing. They fixed your arm. You just have to start being brave."
> Art glared at her. "What do you mean? What makes you think I'm not brave?"

1. What did Art say about a bird with a broken wing? _____

_____

2. Art thinks that he is a bird with a broken wing. What does he mean by that? _____

_____

3. What did Patty tell Art that he should do? _____

4. Art glared at Patty. What does **glare** mean? _____

_____

Part 3

Write these words without endings.

1. watched _____   **5.** skipped _____

2. nodded _____   **6.** feeling _____

3. taken _____   **7.** broken _____

4. making _____   **8.** harder _____

Making deductions, suffixes, compound words

Part 4

Art Feels Sorry for Himself

The cast had been taken from Art's arm. And Art went	11
back to school for the first time. Everybody tried to be friends.	23
At least fifty kids told Art that they were sorry. But Art didn't	36
say much. He just nodded and walked away. He went to his	48
botany class and sat down.	53
Patty was sitting in front of him. She turned around and	64
held up a big red rose. "Here's one that I raised," she said.	77
"What do you think of it?"	83
Art said, "It's pretty. It's very pretty."	90
She smiled and turned back. Art didn't like the way she	101
acted. Why didn't she say, "I'm sorry, Art"?	109
Patty didn't even seem to care. Art would never pitch again,	120
and she didn't even care. After class, he walked up to her in the	134
hall. He didn't know what he would say to her, but he wanted to	148
talk. He wanted to hear her say that she was sorry. Art said, "I	162
had my cast taken off."	167
"I see that," she said.	172
Art said, "The doctor said that I'll never pitch again."	182
She stared at him. Then she asked, "Do you believe that?"	193
"Yes," Art said. "She's a doctor. She should know."	202

A Note to the Parent

Listen to the student read the passage. Count the number of words read in one minute and the number of errors.

Number of words read _____ Number of errors _____

We read the story _____ times.

(Parent's/Listener's) signature _____

Date _____

Reading fluency

Name _____

Part 1

Read the sentences in the box. Then write the answer to each question.

> Now Art was afraid. A player was on third base. There was one out. And Art didn't have a flashing fast ball that would strike out the other batters.
>
> The catcher jogged out and said to Art, "Just make the old brain work, Art. You can strike this next guy out. Just throw the kind of pitch he's not looking for. Watch me. I'll give you some signals."
>
> So Art watched the catcher. The catcher signaled for a slow curve. "No," Art said to himself. "He'll hit it out of the park." Then Art began to think, "Maybe he won't. Maybe he's looking for a very fast ball. Maybe a curve will throw his timing off and make him miss the ball."

1. Art didn't have his flashing fast ball. What is a **flashing** fast ball?

_____

2. What did the catcher tell Art? _____

_____

_____

3. What kind of pitch did the catcher signal for? _____

4. Why could that kind of pitch trick the batter? _____

_____

Part 2

Write the words. Items 1 and 3 are done for you.

1. I   + will = _____ I'll _____

2. he   + will = _____

3. did   + not   = _____ didn't _____

4. would   + not   = _____

5. is   + not   = _____

Conclusions, contractions

Part 3

Patty Challenges Art

Patty was making Art mad. She was trying to get him to	12
skip stones, but he didn't want to. He felt ashamed of himself.	24
Patty picked up a stone and smiled at him. She said, "If	36
you're so bad at skipping stones, I'll bet I could beat you in a	50
contest." She looked out over the pond. She pressed her lips.	61
Then she tossed the stone. "Plunk," it went, and it sank. It	73
didn't skip one time.	77
Art smiled. He said, "That was pretty bad."	85
She said, "I'll do better with this next stone." She picked up	97
the stone, pressed her lips, and gave it a big toss. "Plunk."	109
Art laughed. Then he said, "You're not throwing the right	119
way. You've got to get your arm down low so that you can skim	133
the stone across the water."	138
She picked up another stone and held her arm to her side.	150
"Like this?" she asked.	154
"Sort of," Art said.	158
She made a face and tossed the stone. It skipped once.	169
"There," she said. "Let's see you beat that."	177
Art laughed. "That wouldn't be very hard to beat." He	187
picked up a stone. He leaned to the side. His arm felt stiff and	201
funny when he went to whip it back.	209

A Note to the Parent

Listen to the student read the passage. Count the number of words read in one minute and the number of errors.

Number of words read _____   Number of errors _____

We read the story _____ times.

(Parent's/Listener's) signature _____

Date _____

Reading fluency

Name _____

Part 1

Write these words with **er** endings.

1. speak _____

2. pitch _____

3. fast _____

4. bat _____

Part 2

Write these words with **ing** endings.

1. talk _____

2. start _____

3. stop _____

4. think _____

Part 3

Read the sentences in the box. Then write the answer to each question.

> The president was standing next to the cab. He said to the con man, "Get out of that cab this instant."
>
> The con man got out of the cab. He was thinking to himself, "I must find a way to get away from this guy."
>
> The president said, "Before we leave on our trip, we must find some fine duds. Who would think of going on a trip without fine duds?"

1. The president told the con man to get out of the cab this instant. What does **this instant** mean? _____

2. What does the con man want to do? _____

_____

3. What are **fine duds?** _____

Part 4

Write these words without endings.

1. driver _____ 4. escaped _____

2. faking _____ 5. smiled _____

3. taken _____ 6. grabbed _____

Suffixes, conclusions

Part 5

The Smartest Pitcher

Art became better, but it seemed very slow to him. After	11
working for two months, Art could hardly throw a stone	21
halfway across the pond. After six months, he could throw a	32
stone a little more than halfway across the pond. After almost	43
a year, he could make a stone skip pretty far—but not nearly as	57
far as he had before he'd broken his arm.	66
Art went out for baseball the next spring. The first time	77
he was on the pitcher's mound, the boys on the team yelled,	89
"Come on, Art. Set that catcher on his seat."	98
Art heaved the ball just as hard as he could, but the catcher	111
didn't go down. Art didn't have the same fast ball that he had	124
before. The catcher didn't drop his mitt and blow on his hand	136
after catching one of Art's fast balls.	143
Art wanted to quit the team after that first day. But when he	156
was in the locker room, the coach came up to him. The coach	169
sat down next to him and said, "Art, let's look at the facts. You	183
don't have that flashing fast ball that you had before. But you	195
can still become a good pitcher."	201

A Note to the Parent

Listen to the student read the passage. Count the number of words read in one minute and the number of errors.

Number of words read _____ Number of errors _____

We read the story _____ times.

(Parent's/Listener's) signature _____

Date _____

Reading fluency

Lesson 16

Name _____

Part 1

Write the words. Item 1 is done for you.

1. he   + is   = _____he's_____   4. I   + will = _____

2. there + is   = _____   5. did + not = _____

3. you + will = _____   6. has + not = _____

Part 2

Read the words in the box. Then fill in the blanks.

started	mistake	watched	list	past
pitched	picked	stormed	fuss	mess
guys	shocked	stared	bags	expected
strokes	lies	dashed	tried	desk

The president looked _____. He _____ at the list of names.

Then he said, "I am sorry for making such a _____. I was so upset about our

_____ that I must have looked right _____ the name on the list."

The president was telling _____ left and right. He had just

_____ the name Henry Reeves from the _____ and had given it

to the con man.

Part 3

Write these words with ly endings.

1. proud _____

2. slow _____

3. clean _____

Part 4

Write these words with ing endings.

1. wait _____

2. ship _____

3. catch _____

Contractions, vocabulary/context clues, suffixes

Part 5

A Ride to the Docks

The con man and the president had escaped from the hotel.	11
They were in a cab. The con man had gotten rid of his wig and	26
his bridal dress. He was thinking, "The president is very odd. I	38
must leave and hide somewhere."	43
The president said to the cab driver, "Take us to the docks.	55
We are going to take a trip on a ship because we want to leave	70
this town."	72
So the cab went to the docks. Then the driver said, "That	84
will be six dollars."	88
The president turned to the con man. "Private," he said,	98
"pay the driver."	101
The con man said, "I don't have any cash. But you have two	114
hundred dollars."	116
The president said, "Yes, yes. So I do."	124
Then he reached into his pockets. "I can't seem to find my	136
cash," he said after a moment. The president was faking. He	147
said, "Stay here. I'll be back in a flash with the cash."	159
The president left the cab and walked up to a woman who	171
looked very rich. The president said, "Where is your pass?"	181
The woman looked at the president and blinked. "What	190
pass? I don't know what you're talking about."	198
The president said, "I'm a security officer."	205

A Note to the Parent

Listen to the student read the passage. Count the number of words read in one minute and the number of errors.

Number of words read _____ Number of errors _____

We read the story _____ times.

(Parent's/Listener's) signature _____

Date _____

Reading fluency

Name _____

Part 1   Write the words.

1. with   +   out   =   _____

2. over   +   sight   =   _____

3. every   +   body   =   _____

4. some   +   where   =   _____

Part 2   Read the sentences in the box. Then write the answer to each question.

> As the woman called the shipping department, the president turned to the con man and whispered, "I don't want to tell them that I am a president. That would scare them. So I'll just pretend that I'm another person."
>
> The steamship woman said, "I'm happy to report that all of your bags are safe in our shipping department."
>
> The president turned to the con man and said, "You fool. You told me that our bags were not in the shipping department. You must try to take more care when I give you a task to do."
>
> The con man didn't say a thing. He just looked at the president. The con man said to himself, "If I am a con man, the president is a super con man."

1. What did the woman say about the bags? _____

_____

2. What did the president do next? _____

_____

3. What did the con man think of the president? _____

_____

Part 3   Write these words without endings.

1. hopped   _____   4. turned   _____

2. hopes   _____   5. missing   _____

3. taken   _____   6. hardly   _____

Compound words, details, suffixes

Part 4

Name _____

Sir Robert Fredrick

The president and the con man were at the docks. The	11
president had two hundred and ten dollars. He had gotten two	22
hundred dollars from the hotel by telling the clerk in the hotel	34
that there were bugs in the bridal rooms. When he and the con	47
man went to the docks, the president had gotten twenty dollars	58
from a rich woman. He had given ten dollars to the cab driver.	71
Now the president and the con man were walking along the	82
docks. The con man asked, "Where are we going?"	91
The president said, "Will you stop asking foolish questions!	100
We're going on a trip. I need a good rest at sea."	112
"But . . . ," the con man started to say.	119
"Private, if you ever want to become anything but a private,	130
you must remember to take orders. Just do what I tell you	142
to do."	144
The president and the con man went up to a shop. Over	156
the door of the shop were these words: JAPAN STEAMSHIP	166
LINES.	167
The president stormed into the shop. He dashed up to the	178
woman at the desk and said, "Just what kind of a line are you	192
running? They tell me that my bags are not here yet."	203

A Note to the Parent

Listen to the student read the passage. Count the number of words read in one minute and the number of errors.

Number of words read _____   Number of errors _____

We read the story _____ times.

(Parent's/Listener's) signature _____

Date _____

Reading fluency

Name _____

Part 1

Read the passage and answer the questions.

> A tall man had found out that the con man was trying to steal his bags. The con man was trying to think of something to say, but the words were not flowing from his mouth. He was stammering and stuttering and saying, "You know—I mean, you see. . . ." The tall man was getting very mad.
>
> Then suddenly the president came back. He had a cop with him. He said, "There he is, officer. That tall man is the impostor. Go ask him his name, and you'll see."
>
> The cop went up to the tall man. "All right, buddy," he said. "What's your name?" "Fredrick. Robert Fredrick," the tall man said. "And this man seems to be stealing my bags."

1. What did the president tell the cop? _____

_____

2. What did the tall man say his name was? _____

3. What did the tall man say was going on? _____

_____

Part 2

Write these words without endings.

1. rubbed   _____   5. piped   _____

2. nosed   _____   6. lonely   _____

3. opening   _____   7. shouted   _____

4. quickly   _____   8. flowing   _____

Details, suffixes

Part 3

A Cartload of Bags

The president and the con man were in the office of the	12
Japan Steamship Lines. The president was telling lies so fast	22
that the con man couldn't keep up with him. The president	33
had looked at the names of those who were going on a ship	46
to Japan. He had picked two names. Then he had told the	58
woman behind the desk that one of the names belonged to the	70
president. Now the woman behind the desk was saying that she	81
would help the president find his bags.	88
The woman said, "I will make a call to our shipping	99
department and see if we can locate your bags."	108
As the woman called the shipping department, the president	117
turned to the con man and whispered, "I don't want to tell	129
them that I am a president. That would scare them. So I'll just	142
pretend that I'm another person."	147
The steamship woman said, "I'm happy to report that all of	158
your bags are safe in our shipping department."	166
The president turned to the con man and said, "You fool.	177
You told me that our bags were not in the shipping department.	189
You must try to take more care when I give you a task to do."	204

A Note to the Parent

Listen to the student read the passage. Count the number of words read in one minute and the number of errors.

Number of words read _____ Number of errors _____

We read the story _____ times.

(Parent's/Listener's) signature _____

Date _____

Lesson 19

Name _____

Part 1

Follow the instructions for each exercise.

1. Write the word **partner.** Make a line over **ar.** _____

2. Write the word **person.** Make a line over **er.** _____

3. Write the word **loaded.** Make a line under **oa.** _____

Part 2

Read the words in the box. Then fill in the blanks.

crying	slept	homesick	stammer	plan
spent	hollow	open	start	hollered
demand	crouch	smiling	guy	care
buddy	escape	different	stared	conned

"I have _____ three years at Happy Hollow," the president said. He was

still _____. "Those were the best three years of my life. When the cop said,

'Happy Hollow,' I became _____."

The con man was thinking that he would have to _____ all over. He

would have to _____ some way to get out of the rest home. He said to

himself, "The next time I _____, I won't be _____ into going

with a _____ like the president."

Part 3

Write the words. Item 1 is done for you.

1. they + had = __they'd__   4. I   + will = _____

2. I   + had = _____   5. could + not = _____

3. you   + had = _____   6. here   + is   = _____

Sound/symbol correspondence, vocabulary/context clues, contractions

Part 4

President Washington Tells the Truth

A tall man had found out that the con man was trying to	13
steal his bags. The con man was trying to think of something	25
to say, but the words were not flowing from his mouth. He was	38
stammering and stuttering and saying, "You know—I mean,	47
you see . . ." The tall man was getting very mad.	56
Then suddenly the president came back. He had a cop	66
with him. He said, "There he is, officer. That tall man is the	79
impostor. Go ask him his name, and you'll see."	88
The cop went up to the tall man. "All right, buddy," he said.	101
"What's your name?"	104
"Fredrick. Robert Fredrick," the tall man said. "And this	113
man seems to be stealing my bags."	120
The cop asked, "Do you have identification to show who	130
you are?"	132
"Yes," the tall man said. He reached in his pocket and	143
grabbed his wallet. As he opened it, the president said, "Just	154
as I told you, officer. That man stole my wallet, and now he's	167
trying to steal our bags."	172
The cop turned to the tall man. "All right, buddy," he said.	184
"Hand over the wallet."	188
"I will not!" the man shouted. "That is my wallet."	198

A Note to the Parent

Listen to the student read the passage. Count the number of words read in one minute and the number of errors.

Number of words read _____   Number of errors _____

We read the story _____ times.

(Parent's/Listener's) signature _____

Date _____

Reading fluency

Name _____

Part 1

Write the two words that make up each word.

everything   =   _____   +   _____

homesick   =   _____   +   _____

understand   =   _____   +   _____

without   =   _____   +   _____

Part 2

Read the sentences in the box. Then write the answer to each question.

> Hurn tried to back away from the big cat. But he felt the hard rock of the cave against his back. He could go back no more. Surt was curled next to him.
>
> Without knowing why he did it, Hurn showed his teeth and began to growl. He snapped at the air as if to scare the cat away. The cat stopped for an instant, but then it started to come toward the puppies again.

1. Why couldn't Hurn back away from the big cat? _____

_____

2. Name three things Hurn did to try to scare the cat away. _____

_____

3. What did the cat do next? _____

_____

Part 3

Write these words without endings.

1. smelling   _____   5. snapped   _____

2. smiles   _____   6. noses   _____

3. closer   _____   7. catcher   _____

4. flashing   _____   8. cheering   _____

Compound words, details, suffixes

Lesson 20   **39**

Part 4

Why Did He Tell the Truth?

When the cops said that they were taking the tall man to the	13
Happy Hollow Rest Home, the president began to tell them the	24
truth about everything.	27
The president was saying, "Yes, the tall man is telling the	38
truth. We were trying to con him out of his bags and his wallet.	52
We have also conned the woman at the steamship line out of	64
two fares to Japan. We conned a rich woman out of twenty	76
dollars, and we conned a hotel out of two hundred dollars and	88
a meal for two. There is more if you want to hear about it."	102
The cops let go of the tall man. They stared at the president.	115
The president said, "You must understand that we had to do	126
those things. We are not common crooks. As president, I had to	138
get to Japan. But now things are different."	146
The cops looked at each other. Then they looked at the con	158
man and the president. One cop asked, "What should we do	169
with these guys?"	172
The tall man said, "You may start by giving me my wallet. I	185
don't wish to be late for my trip to Japan."	195
The cop gave the tall man his wallet.	203

A Note to the Parent

Listen to the student read the passage. Count the number of words read in one minute and the number of errors.

Number of words read _____ Number of errors _____

We read the story _____ times.

(Parent's/Listener's) signature _____

Date _____

Reading fluency

Part 1

Write the words. Item 1 is done for you.

1. I + have = _____I've_____   4. there + is = _____

2. you + have = _____   5. you + will = _____

3. did + not = _____   6. is + not = _____

Part 2

Read the sentences in the box. Then write the answer to each question.

> The pups stood in the cold water, shivering and scanning the air with their noses. Slowly the pups walked from the water. But they did not go back to the cave. Something told them that the cave was no longer safe. Something said to Hurn, "Stay away from the cave."
>
> So Hurn and Surt began to follow the bank of the stream. Hurn led the way. Surt followed. From time to time she tried to play with her brother, but Hurn wouldn't play.

1. When the pups stood in the water, what did they do with their noses?

_____

2. Why didn't the pups go back to the cave? _____

_____

3. Where did the pups go after they got out of the stream? _____

_____

4. Which wolf pup still wanted to play? _____

Part 3

Match the words and complete them.

_____ quickly _____ •   • _____ er _____

_____ shivering _____ •   • _____ ir _____

_____ reached _____ •   • _____ ck _____

_____ wheeze _____ •   • _____ ch _____

_____ thirsty _____ •   • _____ ee _____

Contractions, details, word match

Name _____

Part 4

Hurn, the Wolf

Hurn was sleeping when it happened. Hurn didn't hear the	10
big cat sneak into the cave that Hurn called his home. Suddenly	22
Hurn was awake. Something told him, "Beware!" His eyes	31
turned to the darkness near the mouth of the cave. Hurn felt	43
the fur on the back of his neck stand up. His nose, like noses	57
of all wolves, was very keen. It made him very happy when it	70
smelled something good. But now it smelled something that	79
made him afraid.	82
Hurn was five months old. He had never seen a big cat. He	95
had seen clover and ferns and grass. He had even eaten rabbits.	107
Hurn's mother had come back with them after she had been	118
hunting. She had always come back. And Hurn had always	128
been glad to see her. But now she was not in the cave. Hurn's	142
sister, Surt, was the only happy smell that reached Hurn's nose.	153
Surt was awake. She was leaning against Hurn, and Hurn	163
could feel how hard Surt was shaking.	170
"Oooooooowww," howled Surt. At the sound of the howl,	179
Hurn jerked. Then he turned his nose back toward the mouth of	191
the cave. He made his ears stand up as high as they would go.	205

A Note to the Parent

Listen to the student read the passage. Count the number of words read in one minute and the number of errors.

Number of words read _____ Number of errors _____

We read the story _____ times.

(Parent's/Listener's) signature _____

Date _____

Reading fluency

Name _____

Part 1
Write the words.

1. sudden + ly = _____

2. howl + ed = _____

3. long + er = _____

4. time + s = _____

5. reach + es = _____

Part 2
Read the words in the box. Then fill in the blanks.

curled	toward	fell	staring	stepped
fire	dash	care	ferns	crouched
roasting	rustling	rising	reached	burned
chunk	turning	jumped	hurry	might

Suddenly there was a _____ sound in the _____ next to

Hurn. Hurn turned. The sound came from Surt. She was running _____ the

spit. She was running as fast as her legs would take her. She _____

the spit before any of the men saw her, and she might have gotten away with a big

_____ of deer meat—except for one thing. She _____ in the fire.

She had never seen fire before. She had been in such a _____ to get the meat

that she didn't take as much _____ as she should have.

Part 3
Write these words without endings.

1. tossed _____   5. broken _____

2. softly _____   6. takes _____

3. shines _____   7. hunter _____

4. following _____   8. popped _____

Suffixes, vocabulary/context clues

Part 4

The Hunter's Camp

Hurn's mother had been in a fight with a big cat. She scared	13
the cat from the cave, but the cat had won the fight. Hurn's	26
mother died that night.	30
At first, Hurn cried and howled. He prodded his mother	40
with his nose. He gave her a little bite on her ear. But she lay	55
still. So Hurn cried and howled.	61
Surt cried, too. For most of the day, they stayed by their	73
mother. They didn't go out to run after butterflies. They didn't	84
chase rabbits. They didn't even want to go to the stream for a	97
drink and a cool swim. They sat near their mother and waited	109
for her to get up. But she didn't get up.	119
When the afternoon sun was getting near the tops of the fir	131
trees, Surt walked over to Hurn and bit him on the tail. In an	145
instant, Hurn turned around and bit his sister on the throat. It	157
was a play bite, but it was the kind of bite that big wolves give	172
when they are hunting.	176
Soon Surt and her brother were rolling and churning on	186
the ground. For a moment, Hurn was happy, but the moment	197
passed quickly. As suddenly as the pups had started playing,	207
they stopped and sat.	211

A Note to the Parent

Listen to the student read the passage. Count the number of words read in one minute and the number of errors.

Number of words read _____   Number of errors _____

We read the story _____ times.

(Parent's/Listener's) signature _____

Date _____

Reading fluency

Name _____

Part 1

Read the words in the box. Then fill in the blanks.

something	pat	water	walking	playing
sniffing	slowly	brother	fiddle	somewhere
smelling	friend	trumpet	three	poke
mother	limping	quickly	all	push

As the man played the _____, Surt began to walk _____

down the hill toward the men. She was still _____, but she walked on

_____ of her paws. She walked over to Vern and sat down next to him. The

men did not see her do this.

Surt sniffed the air. She was _____ the meat. She wanted some more meat,

but she wanted _____ else, too. She missed her _____. She

wanted a friend. So she leaned over and gave Vern a little _____ with her nose.

Part 2

Read the sentences in the box. Then write the answer to each question.

> One of the men was stirring the beans. Another was sitting near the spit. Vern sat on the other side of the fire. And Hurn was trying to hear everything and see everything. But he didn't move. The only things that moved were his sides as he breathed.

1. Who was stirring the beans? _____

2. Where was Vern? _____

3. Hurn stayed very still. What part of him moved? _____

_____

4. Why do you think Hurn didn't move? _____

_____

Vocabulary/context clues, details

Part 3

Surt Goes for the Meat

Surt was running toward the hunters' camp. Hurn was	9
following. As Hurn rounded a bend in the stream, he could see	21
a swirl of smoke rising from the campfire. A man was bent over	34
the fire, stirring a pot of beans. Next to the beans was a deer	48
leg roasting on a spit. Another hunter was turning the spit. The	60
men were talking.	63
"Did you see the marks on that cat?" one man said. "It	75
looked like that cat was in a whale of a fight."	86
"That cat was in such bad shape that it dropped before you	98
shot it," another hunter said. He and a third man began to laugh.	111
The first man said, "Come on, you guys. That was a good	123
shot."	124
Hurn hid behind a fern. His mouth was watering. He was	135
staring at the deer leg on the spit. He wanted to dash over to	149
the spit and grab it and take a big bite from it. But he looked	164
and waited.	166
"Hey, Herb," one of the men yelled. "How long before those	177
beans are ready? I'm getting mighty hungry."	184
"Look, Vern, if you want to fix the beans, you can take over	197
any time you want."	201

A Note to the Parent

Listen to the student read the passage. Count the number of words read in one minute and the number of errors.

Number of words read _____ Number of errors _____

We read the story _____ times.

(Parent's/Listener's) signature _____

Date _____

Reading fluency

Name _____

Part 1

Write these words without endings.

1. wagged   _____   5. howling   _____

2. softly   _____   6. followed   _____

3. stepping   _____   7. watched   _____

4. piled   _____   8. sitting   _____

Part 2

Read the sentences in the box. Then write the answer to each question.

> Hurn wanted to curl up and sleep. He wanted to dream about eating or running or chasing butterflies. But when he was done with his drink, he began walking upstream along the bank of the stream.
>
> He felt like going back to the cave, but he didn't remember how to get to the cave. And he remembered that the cave was not his home any more. He had to find a new cave. He had to find a friend. So he walked and walked.

1. What did Hurn do after he had a drink at the stream? _____

_____

2. Why didn't he go back to the cave? _____

_____

3. Name two things Hurn needed to do. _____

_____

Part 3

Write the two words that make up each part.

1. didn't   =   _____   +   _____

2. I'll   =   _____   +   _____

3. here's   =   _____   +   _____

Suffixes, details, contractions

    Lesson 24   **47**

Part 4

Surt and Vern

Hurn was watching from behind a fern. He saw the man	11
called Vern give a chunk of meat to Surt. He saw Surt eat the	25
meat. Hurn crouched down low as the other men came back	36
from the stream. When they reached the campfire, Surt ran	46
away on three legs. She held one leg high. That was the leg that	60
had been burned when Surt stepped in the fire.	69
"Grab it, Vern," one of the men yelled.	77
Vern said, "Let it go. Do you have to kill everything you	89
see?"	90
Surt did not run back toward Hurn. She began running up	101
the hill on the far side of the camp.	110
When Surt was about eighty feet from the men, she stopped	121
and looked back. Then she sat down and began to lick her sore	134
paw.	135
Vern cut another chunk of meat from the roast and walked	146
over to Surt. Slowly Vern bent down and held out the meat.	158
"Are you still hungry?" Vern asked.	164
At first, Surt laid her ears back and curled up her lip. But	177
then her ears began to stand up again. Vern was very still. And	190
so was Surt. Surt sniffed the meat. Then she slowly took it in	203
her mouth.	205

A Note to the Parent

Listen to the student read the passage. Count the number of words read in one minute and the number of errors.

Number of words read _____   Number of errors _____

We read the story _____ times.

(Parent's/Listener's) signature _____

Date _____

Reading fluency

Name _____

Part 1
Write the words.

1. stiff + ly = _____

2. tug + ed = _____

3. whine + ed = _____

4. scan + ing = _____

5. miss + ed = _____

6. stare + ing = _____

Part 2
Read the words in the box. Then fill in the blanks.

nipped	followed	closed	beat	yawned
ran	eat	sniffed	dashed	snuggled
harm	standing	opening	sneaked	tired
back	blinked	howled	stared	realized

Hurn _____ the tan wolf back to her den. There he met her pup. He

was sleeping, curled up in a little ball. Hurn _____ him, and the tan wolf

_____ at Hurn. When she felt that Hurn would not _____ her

pup, she _____. Then she turned around three times and lay down with her

nose toward the _____ of the den.

Hurn _____ up next to her. They looked like two balls of fur. Hurn was so,

so tired. He _____ two times. Then his eyes closed, and he went to sleep.

Suffixes, vocabulary/context clues

Hurn Is Alone

Surt had tried to make friends with Vern. The other men	11
hadn't seen Surt walk down the hill and come over to Vern.	23
Now Vern was patting Surt, and Surt's tail was wagging.	33
One of the other men turned around. "Hey, what's going	43
on?" he snapped. "You can't make friends with that wolf. Get it	55
out of here."	58
Vern said, "Look, Bert, did you ever ask yourself what a	69
wolf this old is doing out at night all by itself? Wolves this old	83
are with their mothers—when they have mothers. I'll bet this	94
little wolf doesn't have a mother."	100
"So what?" Bert said. "Wolves are no good. They kill other	111
animals."	112
Vern said, "When wolves aren't around, things get out of	122
whack. Too many of the other animals live. Then we have real	134
problems."	135
Bert said, "Well, keep that thing away from me. I hate	146
wolves."	147
At that moment, something told Hurn to leave. Something	156
told him that Surt was no longer his sister. Hurn was right, but	169
he didn't know it then. Vern would keep Surt, and Surt would	181
become as tame as most dogs. She would live with Vern, and she	194
would love Vern almost as much as she had loved her mother.	206

A Note to the Parent

Listen to the student read the passage. Count the number of words read in one minute and the number of errors.

Number of words read _____ Number of errors _____

We read the story _____ times.

(Parent's/Listener's) signature _____

Date _____

Reading fluency

Name _____

Part 1

Read the sentences in the box. Then write the answer to each question.

> Then the tan wolf began to walk up the slope, past the other wolves. When she was part way up the slope, she stopped and waited for Hurn. He ran up behind her and tried to hide under her. She held her head up and walked on past the other wolves. They stared at her as she passed.

1. How did the tan wolf show that she wanted Hurn to follow her? _____

_____

2. Why did Hurn try to hide under her? _____

_____

3. What did the other wolves do as the tan wolf walked past them? _____

_____

Part 2

Write the two words that make up each word.

1. outside = _____ + _____

2. daytime = _____ + _____

3. campfire = _____ + _____

4. someday = _____ + _____

5. upwind = _____ + _____

Part 3

Write the two words that make up each word.

1. you'll = _____ + _____

2. isn't = _____ + _____

3. I've = _____ + _____

Inferences, compound words, contractions

Name _____

Part 4

The Tan Wolf

Hurn had been walking along the stream all night. Then he	11
had stopped and begun to howl. He stopped howling when he	22
felt that something was watching.	27
And there was something that was watching him. It was	37
a big tan wolf. She was less than ten feet from Hurn. She had	51
come down to the stream when Hurn first began to howl. She	63
had left her pup asleep in a hollow just below a cliff. And she	77
had sneaked down.	80
Now she was standing behind a fir tree, looking at Hurn.	91
She was upwind from him. Like all good hunters, she moved so	103
that the breeze was blowing toward her. The breeze was blowing	114
from Hurn toward the tan wolf. That way, Hurn couldn't smell	125
her.	126
That tan wolf didn't know what to make of Hurn. She knew	138
that he wasn't a grown wolf. Her nose told her that. But she also	152
knew that he wasn't one of her pups. She missed her pups. She	165
had given birth to six pups. That was three months back. All of	178
the pups but one had died. She missed them, but she knew that	191
Hurn was not hers. And yet—she wanted another pup.	201

A Note to the Parent

Listen to the student read the passage. Count the number of words read in one minute and the number of errors.

Number of words read _____ Number of errors _____

We read the story _____ times.

(Parent's/Listener's) signature _____

Date _____

Reading fluency

Lesson 27

Name _____

Part 1

Read the sentences in the box and answer the questions.

> The fox was very smart. It would bite off bits of fur and drop them on the bank of the stream. Then the fox would swim to the other side of the stream. The idea was to get the wolves mixed up.
>
> And the plan almost worked. The wolves came to the bank of the stream. They smelled the bits of fur. The smell was very strong. It was so strong that the wolves could smell nothing else. They ran around and around, but they always came back to the bits of fur.

1. What did the fox do to trick the wolves? _____

_____

2. Why did the bits of fur fool the wolves? _____

_____

3. Where was the fox? _____

Part 2

Write the words.

1. smart   +   er   =   _____
2. roll   +   ed   =   _____
3. jog   +   ed   =   _____
4. gaze   +   ed   =   _____
5. chase   +   ing   =   _____
6. quick   +   ly   =   _____

Part 3

Write the words.

1. could   +   not   =   _____
2. you   +   had   =   _____
3. there   +   is   =   _____

Details, suffixes, contractions

Hurn Meets the Wolf Pack

Hurn slept like a log that night. He woke up once when the	13
tan wolf left the den, but he went back to sleep in a moment.	27
When he woke up the next time, the sun was high in the sky.	41
The air was almost hot, and things looked so bright outside the	53
den that Hurn blinked. The tan wolf was not around, nor was	65
her pup.	67
Hurn walked from the den, and then he stopped. There was	78
a big, black wolf standing on the slope. That wolf was looking	90
at Hurn. Another wolf, a brown one, was also looking at Hurn.	102
Far on the other side of the clearing were the tan wolf and her	116
pup.	117
Something told Hurn to stay away from the other wolves, so	128
he began to walk toward the tan wolf. Then he began to run.	141
Hurn didn't know that the tan wolf was part of a wolf	153
pack. There were 8 wolves in the pack. The tan wolf had kept	166
to herself for a time after she had her pups. Any grown wolf	179
who came near her den was asking for a good fight. The tan	192
wolf could beat up any wolf in the pack except the black wolf.	205
No wolf messed with him.	210

A Note to the Parent

Listen to the student read the passage. Count the number of words read in one minute and the number of errors.

Number of words read _____   Number of errors _____

We read the story _____ times.

(Parent's/Listener's) signature _____

Date _____

Reading fluency

Part 1

Read the words in the box. Then fill in the blanks.

hill	best	piled	summer	trick	plants	winner
black	fall	boss	tan	animals	ground	easy
hard	winter	mountain	fish	drifts	bite	backed
fight	brown	stacks	swirled			

Hurn didn't have to _____ any of the other wolves. They seemed to know that Hurn

was _____. Maybe they knew from the way he had gone at the _____ wolf.

Late in the fall, Hurn led the other wolves to high _____, way up the side of a

_____. They would spend the _____ up there, and they would not have

an _____ time. The trees were not tall, and there were not many _____.

The snow came early. It _____ down every night. Before the middle of December,

the snow had _____ up in _____ that were twenty feet high.

Part 2

Write the two words that make up each word.

1. hasn't   =   _____   +   _____

2. I'll   =   _____   +   _____

3. you've   =   _____   +   _____

4. wouldn't   =   _____   +   _____

Part 3

Write the words.

1. loud   +   est   =   _____

2. get   +   ing   =   _____

3. fool   +   ed   =   _____

4. puzzle   +   ed   =   _____

5. near   +   ly   =   _____

Vocabulary/context clues, contractions, suffixes

Name _____

Part 4

Things Change for Hurn

Hurn had lived with the tan wolf for nearly a year. She had	13
been like a mother to him. He loved her. That is why he was so	28
puzzled that day when he came back to the den. He had been	41
hunting with some of the other wolves. Hurn was getting to be	53
a fair hunter. He had helped the pack bring down a small deer.	66
He had hunted for rabbits and pack rats. Hurn was feeling more	78
like a grown wolf every day. He jogged up the path to his den,	92
just as he had many times before.	99
But when he got near the den, the tan wolf met him. She	112
gazed at him in a funny way. Hurn stopped. Then he began to	125
walk toward her. She crouched down and showed her teeth.	135
"Grrr," she growled.	138
She was trying to tell Hurn something, but he didn't get	149
what it was. She was trying to say, "I am going to have pups in	164
a day or two. That means that you must leave. No more are you	178
a pup. No more are you welcome in this den."	188
She didn't look as if she wanted to play, but Hurn began to	201
think that maybe she wanted to play.	208

A Note to the Parent

Listen to the student read the passage. Count the number of words read in one minute and the number of errors.

Number of words read _____   Number of errors _____

We read the story _____ times.

(Parent's/Listener's) signature _____

Date _____

Reading fluency

Name _____

Part 1

Write these words without endings.

1. slowly   _____

2. crouched   _____

3. rubbed   _____

4. bothered   _____

5. starved   _____

6. friendly   _____

7. piles   _____

8. chasing   _____

Part 2

Read the sentences in the box. Then write the answer to each question.

> Hurn didn't walk away from the wolf pup. Hurn got above the wolf pup and grabbed her by the nape of the neck. He gave a hard jerk. The pup let out a yelp, but now the pup was free. The pup wagged her tail and rolled over on her back to show Hurn that he was boss and that she would do what he wanted her to do.

1. What did Hurn do to the wolf pup? _____

_____

2. The pup let out a yelp. What is a **yelp?** _____

3. Why did the pup roll over on her back? _____

_____

Part 3

Write the words.

1. he   +   is   =   _____

2. is   +   not   =   _____

3. you   +   have   =   _____

4. here   +   is   =   _____

Suffixes, details, contractions

Name _____

Part 4

The Fight

The fox had a trick that almost worked, but the black wolf	12
was not fooled. He did not run around and around like Hurn	24
and the other wolves. He walked to the middle of the stream.	36
He held his nose high and stood there for a long time. He was	50
trying to get a fresh smell from the air. At last he did. He swam	65
to the other side of the stream. He howled to let the other	78
wolves know that he had found the trail.	86
The wolves had a good meal that night. But there weren't as	98
many good meals as there had been last year.	107
The pack was getting too big. Some of the wolves would	118
have to leave. Hurn didn't know it, but he was one of those	131
wolves. The brown wolf, Hurn, and two other wolves would not	142
go back with the pack that night.	149
When the wolves had eaten the fox, the black wolf walked	160
over and bit the brown wolf. The brown wolf howled but he	172
didn't fight back. Then the black wolf bit Hurn. Hurn did not	184
howl. The fur on Hurn's back stood up, and Hurn began to	196
fight with the black wolf.	201

A Note to the Parent Listen to the student read the passage. Count the number of words read in one minute and the number of errors.

Number of words read _____ Number of errors _____

We read the story _____ times.

(Parent's/Listener's) signature _____

Date _____

Reading fluency

Lesson 30

Name _____

Part 1

Match the words and complete them.

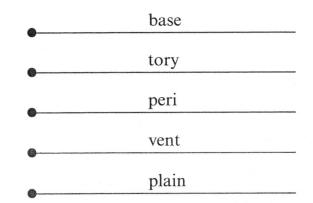

inventor ● ● base

experiment ● ● tory

basement ● ● peri

complain ● ● vent

factory ● ● plain

Part 2

1. Write the word **lousy.** Make a line over the **ou.** _____

2. Write the word **point.** Make a line under the **oi.** _____

3. Write the word **boarding.** Make a line over the **oa.** _____

4. Write the word **toil.** Make a line under the **oi.** _____

5. Write the word **folded.** Make a line under the **ol.** _____

Part 3
Write the words.

1. like   + ed   = _____

2. bright + ly   = _____

3. invent + or   = _____

4. board + ing   = _____

5. starve + ed   = _____

Part 4
Write the words.

1. some   + body = _____

2. may   + be   = _____

3. with   + out   = _____

4. every   + one   = _____

5. an   + other = _____

Word match, word parts, suffixes, compound words

Name _____

Part 5

The Leader of the Pack

As Hurn and the other wolves slowly walked down the side	11
of the mountain, a big black bear came out of its den. The	24
bear had been sleeping nearly all winter, and it was mean and	36
hungry. The bear stood up and growled at the wolves. They	47
turned and began to walk away.	53
The bear was not in a friendly mood. "Grrrrr," it growled,	64
and started to chase Hurn and the other wolves.	73
Down the mountainside they went. The wolves had to run	83
pretty fast because that bear was fast. The wolves ran about	94
500 yards. They were panting. The bear was panting, too.	104
Suddenly Hurn stopped. The other wolves kept running,	112
but something told Hurn that he would run no more. He would	124
turn around and fight that bear.	130
Wolves fight bears sometimes, but that is rare. Even when	140
wolves are very hungry, they will not bother bears. Sometimes a	151
big pack of wolves will attack a bear, but wolves must be almost	164
starved before they'll do that. Hurn was hungry, but he wasn't	175
almost starved. And he didn't plan to fight with the help of	187
other wolves. He just didn't want to run from that bear any	199
more.	200

A Note to the Parent

Listen to the student read the passage. Count the number of words read in one minute and the number of errors.

Number of words read _____ Number of errors _____

We read the story _____ times.

(Parent's/Listener's) signature _____

Date _____

Reading fluency

Name _____

Part 1
Match the words and complete them.

recall ● ● pret

hammer ● ● call

crazy ● ● fool

pretzel ● ● mer

foolish ● ● y

Part 2
Write the words.

1. listen + ed = _____

2. stick + y = _____

3. drop + ing = _____

4. flat + er = _____

5. walk + ing = _____

6. dent + s = _____

Part 3
Write the two words that make up each word.

1. yourself = _____ + _____

2. downstairs = _____ + _____

3. anything = _____ + _____

4. paintbrush = _____ + _____

5. anyone = _____ + _____

Word match, suffixes, compound words

Part 4

Why Irma Boils

There once was a woman named Irma. Irma ran a boarding	11
house. Seven people lived in her boarding house. They slept in	22
the boarding house, ate in this house, and paid Irma for their	34
rooms and meals. But they did not treat Irma very well.	45
Carl and Herman were brothers who lived on the second	55
floor of the house. Herman worked in an oil plant. Carl toiled	67
in a meat plant. The two brothers did not get along with each	80
other.	81
Berta was a loud woman who lived on the first floor. She	93
didn't have a job. She spent most of her time watching TV.	105
Three women lived on the third floor of Irma's boarding house.	116
All worked in a cheese factory. Irma worked in that factory, too.	128
Every evening, Irma came home very tired. But nobody	137
greeted her at the door with a smile. Herman would usually be	149
standing near the door. He would say, "It's about time you got	161
home. Now go out and get some hamburgers for us to eat. We	174
are starved."	176
So Irma would go out and get the hamburgers. And when	187
she would come back, Berta wouldn't say, "Irma, it's very good	198
of you to get those hamburgers."	204

A Note to the Parent

Listen to the student read the passage. Count the number of words read in one minute and the number of errors.

Number of words read _____ Number of errors _____

We read the story _____ times.

(Parent's/Listener's) signature _____

Date _____

Reading fluency

Lesson 32

Name _____

Part 1

Write the words. Item 1 is done for you.

1. do + not = _____don't_____   4. would + not = _____

2. you + will = _____   5. I + had = _____

3. she + is = _____   6. we + have = _____

Part 2

Write the words without endings.

1. watching   _____   5. smiled   _____

2. wadded   _____   6. dropped   _____

3. chores   _____   7. relatives   _____

4. beaches   _____   8. stinky   _____

Part 3

Write the words.

1. up + stairs = _____   4. how + ever = _____

2. some + thing = _____   5. with + out = _____

3. any + body = _____   6. day + light = _____

Contractions, suffixes, compound words

Part 4

Irma Makes Paint

As you may recall from the last Irma story, Irma was very	12
unhappy. She worked all day in the cheese factory. When she	23
got home, she had to fix meals for her boarders. Then she	35
washed the clothes while they watched TV.	42
When we left Irma, she felt good because she was done with	54
her chores for the day. She could now work on her paint. She	67
went into her lab and closed the door. She could hear the others	80
upstairs laughing.	82
"Go get the pretzels," Carl said to Berta.	90
"Get them yourself, you bum."	95
Irma went to the jars of paint she had been working with.	107
She wanted to see how hard the paint in each jar was. The paint	121
had been drying for almost three days.	128
She tapped the paint in the first jar. It was not hard. There	141
was a film of hard paint on top, but the paint under the film	155
was still wet and sticky.	160
She tapped the paint in the next jar. It was pretty hard, but	173
there was still some soft paint under the film on top.	184
Irma went to the last jar of paint. She tapped it. It was	197
hard. She tapped it harder and harder.	204

A Note to the Parent

Listen to the student read the passage. Count the number of words read in one minute and the number of errors.

Number of words read _____   Number of errors _____

We read the story _____ times.

(Parent's/Listener's) signature _____

Date _____

Reading fluency

Name _____

Part 1

Write the name of the person each sentence tells about.

Herman   **Carl**   **Irma**   **Berta**   **Fern**

1. This person said, "I don't know why we stay here. She is all for herself. She never thinks about anybody else."   _____

2. This person said, "Here is the hand you wanted," and held up her right hand.   _____

3. This person looked at the hand. His lips moved, but his voice did not seem to be working.   _____

4. This person looked at the hand and said, "Uh, buh, duh, buh, buh, uh."   _____

Part 2

Fill in the circle next to the word that completes the sentence. Write the word in the blank.

1. Herman sat on the _____ and watched TV.   ○ coach   ○ couch

2. Irma dumped the _____ from the jar.   ○ paint   ○ point

3. In a _____ voice, she said, "You wanted me to give you a hand?"   ○ lead   ○ loud

4. Fern stopped talking and _____ at the hand.   ○ starred   ○ stared

Part 3

Write the words.

1. wave + ed = _____   4. joke + s = _____

2. bake + ing = _____   5. stop + ed = _____

3. face + ing = _____   6. stare + ed = _____

Characterization, spelling, suffixes

Part 4

Irma Tests the Invisible Paint

Irma had left a nail on the hard paint. When she came back	13
to her lab, the nail was invisible. Slowly she began to realize that	26
the paint had made the nail invisible.	33
She said to herself, "I will test that paint." She took a coin	46
from her purse and dropped the coin on the paint. Then she	58
watched and waited. After a while, she saw that the coin was	70
starting to turn invisible. It now looked like a glass coin. She	82
could still see it, but it did not look like a copper coin or a silver	98
coin. It looked like a glass coin.	105
She dropped it on the floor. "Clink," it went. It sounded	116
like a coin. She took a hammer and hit the coin ten times.	129
She wanted to see what would happen to it now. The coin got	142
flatter and bigger, but it still looked like glass. She said, "I don't	155
believe what is happening."	159
She set the coin on the paint again and waited. Soon the	171
coin was invisible. Now it didn't look like glass. It didn't look	183
like anything.	185
"I don't believe it," Irma said to herself. She felt the coin.	197
She could feel the dents that had been made by the hammer.	209

A Note to the Parent

Listen to the student read the passage. Count the number of words read in one minute and the number of errors.

Number of words read _____   Number of errors _____

We read the story _____ times.

(Parent's/Listener's) signature _____

Date _____

Reading fluency

Lesson 34

Name _____

Part 1
Write these words without endings.

1. stopped   _____   5. glasses   _____

2. hoped   _____   6. tossed   _____

3. waking   _____   7. grabbed   _____

4. staring   _____   8. making   _____

Part 2
Write the words. Item 1 is done for you.

1. does + not = ___doesn't___   4. he + is = _____

2. do + not = _____   5. they + had = _____

3. we + will = _____   6. I + have = _____

Part 3
Fill in the circle next to the word that completes the sentence. Write the word in the blank.

1. Berta ran from the room as fast as a track _____.   ○ stare   ○ star

2. Irma _____ the rag on the invisible paint.   ○ rubbed   ○ robbed

3. Fern was just _____ up again.   ○ walking   ○ waking

Suffixes, contractions, spelling

Part 4

Irma Gives Them a Hand

As you may recall, Irma had made a batch of invisible	11
paint. Then she got an idea about how she could have a lot of	25
fun with that paint.	29
She began to think of all kinds of fun things that she could	42
do. She could rub the paint on herself. Then she could go	54
upstairs and pay back her boarders for being mean to her. She	66
could scare them. She could play jokes on them. She smiled to	78
herself as she began to think about the things she could do.	90
"Irma," Herman yelled. "We are trying to move the couch.	100
Get up here and give us a hand."	108
"Yes," Irma answered. "I'll give you a hand."	116
Quickly she grabbed the jar with the invisible paint in it.	127
She dumped the paint from the jar. Then she began rubbing the	139
paint on herself. She rubbed it on her head, her arms, her body,	152
her legs, and her feet. She rubbed paint on every part of her but	166
her right hand. Then she waited and watched as she became	177
invisible.	178
"Irma, get up here and give us a hand. You can fool around	191
in that stinky basement some other time."	198
Irma looked at herself in the cracked mirror that was in her	210
lab.	211

A Note to the Parent

Listen to the student read the passage. Count the number of words read in one minute and the number of errors.

Number of words read _____   Number of errors _____

We read the story _____ times.

(Parent's/Listener's) signature _____

Date _____

Reading fluency

Name _____

Part 1

Write the words. Items 1, 5, and 9 are done for you.

1. I   + am   = _____I'm_____   6. it   + is   = _____

2. I   + will = _____   7. do   + not = _____

3. he + will = _____   8. does + not = _____

4. she + is   = _____   9. we   + are = _____we're_____

5. he + has = _____he's_____   10. you + are = _____

Part 2

Write these words without endings.

1. flipped   _____   5. offering   _____

2. closed   _____   6. really   _____

3. drapes   _____   7. remarked   _____

4. places   _____   8. smiled   _____

Part 3

Write the two words that make up each word.

1. inside   = _____   + _____

2. herself   = _____   + _____

3. something = _____   + _____

Contractions, suffixes, compound words

Name _____

Part 4

Did They Really Want a Hand?

Irma had come up to give Herman and the others a hand.	12
She had made every part of herself invisible except her right	23
hand. She went to the living room. Then she said, "You wanted	35
a hand? Here it is." She waved the hand around.	45
The others stopped and stared. They were still staring. The	55
man on the TV was saying, "Yes, friends, we have a car for	68
everybody. So come on down to the Car Mart and pick out the	81
car of your dreams."	85
Carl was still saying, "Buh, duh, uh, buh, buh, uh, duh."	96
Then he stopped going, "Buh, duh," and started to say	106
something else. "I'm getting out of . . . I'm getting . . . I'm . . ."	115
Suddenly Carl turned around and took a dive at the	125
window. "Crash," the glass went, and Carl went rolling on the	136
ground outside the window. He got up and ran. He ran like a	149
streak. "I'm getting out of . . . I'm getting . . . ," he yelled.	158
Berta stood there and stared at the hand for a while. Then	170
she said, "Is that hand a hand, or is that hand not a hand?	184
Or is . . . ?"	186
Irma said, "You wanted me to give you a hand, didn't you?"	198

A Note to the Parent

Listen to the student read the passage. Count the number of words read in one minute and the number of errors.

Number of words read _____ Number of errors _____

We read the story _____ times.

(Parent's/Listener's) signature _____

Date _____

Reading fluency

Name _____

Part 1

Read the words in the box. Then fill in the blanks.

grab	meal	scare	fast	anything	chore
mean	right	listen	main	something	now
bold	yell	stand	stare	remember	careful
quiet	next	remarked	note	tone	stand

Irma said, "I have _____ to say, and I am going to say it right now. And I

want you to _____."

"All right, all right," Carl said. "Say what you have to say. Just make it _____."

Irma said, "From now on, don't _____ at me. Don't tell me to do every

_____ around this house. And don't be _____ to me."

Berta said, "Who do you think you are, talking to me in that _____

of voice?"

"You know very well who I am," Irma said. "Just _____ what I'm

telling you."

"Oh, be _____, and let's eat," Carl _____.

Part 2

Write the words.

1. eat   + en = _____

2. bother   + ing = _____

3. boil   + ed = _____

4. complain + ing = _____

5. taco   + s   = _____

6. daze   + ed = _____

7. scare   + ed = _____

8. mix   + ed = _____

Vocabulary/context clues, suffixes

Name _____

Part 3

Looking for the Hand

After Irma had given Herman and the others a "hand," she	11
removed the invisible paint with oil. Then she took a shower	22
and went back to the living room. When Fern saw her, she	34
passed out again.	37
Irma laughed and walked over to the TV set. The same man	49
was still on the TV. He was saying, "Before we return to the	62
movie, let me just show you three or four more of the cars that	76
we are offering as part of our sale."	84
Irma turned off the set. Then she closed the drapes on the	96
window that had been broken when Carl dove out. Then Irma	107
sat down and began to think of other things that she could do.	120
At last, Fern woke up. She was very pale. She sat up and	133
stared at Irma. Then she started to say, "Are you really . . . ?"	144
Just then Carl came in the front door. "Where is that hand?"	156
he asked. He was carrying a bat.	163
Irma held out her hand. "Here it is," she said.	173
"Not that hand," Carl said. "I want the hand that was	184
floating around this room."	188
Irma pointed to her hand. "This is it," she said.	198

A Note to the Parent

Listen to the student read the passage. Count the number of words read in one minute and the number of errors.

Number of words read _____ Number of errors _____

We read the story _____ times.

(Parent's/Listener's) signature _____

Date _____

Reading fluency

Name _____

Part 1

Write the name of the person each sentence tells about.

Irma   **Berta**   **Fern**   **Herman**   **Carl**

1. This person said, "Who has my keys? Give them back
right now."   _____

2. This person said, "Will you cut the noise? I can't even
hear what they're saying on TV."   _____

3. This person was yelling, "I want my keys."   _____

4. This person was yelling, "I hope you can find them, so
that you can get out of here, you bum."   _____

5. This person was yelling, "I don't know anything about
your lousy keys."   _____

6. This person was laughing.   _____

Part 2

Write the words. Items 1 and 3 are done for you.

1. what + is = _____ what's _____   **6.** was + not = _____

2. that + is = _____   **7.** we + are = _____

3. can + not = _____ can't _____   **8.** were + not = _____

4. I + am = _____   **9.** she + has = _____

5. do + not = _____   **10.** you + have = _____

Characterization, contractions

Part 3

Irma Gets Ready

After Irma had scared Carl and the other boarders with the	11
hand, she made up her mind about two things.	20
The first thing was that she wouldn't scare them again,	30
unless they were mean to her.	36
The second was that she would make another batch of	46
paint, a big batch.	50
For the next three or four days, everyone was pretty nice	61
to Irma. They weren't really nice. They just weren't bothering	71
her as much as they had. In fact, they didn't say much. They	84
seemed to be dazed.	88
Before Irma had scared them, Carl had eaten like a goat.	99
But now he wouldn't even finish one helping. Before Herman	109
had been scared, he had spent more time complaining than	119
eating. But now he just picked at his food without saying much.	131
And after dinner, Fern and Berta went into the living room	142
and sat. Sometimes they would not remember to turn on the	153
TV set. They just sat and stared at the set.	163
Irma got a lot done on those days. Right after dinner, she	175
would go down to the lab and work on her paint. She boiled	188
sheep fat. The smell was bad, but nobody yelled, "Stop making	199
that stink down there."	203

A Note to the Parent

Listen to the student read the passage. Count the number of words read in one minute and the number of errors.

Number of words read _____ Number of errors _____

We read the story _____ times.

(Parent's/Listener's) signature _____

Date _____

Reading fluency

Name _____

Part 1

Read the sentences in the box and answer the questions.

> Irma had done some things to start an argument between her boarders. She had removed Carl's keys from his coat and slipped them into Herman's pocket. She had taken a glass and placed it next to Carl. Then she had taken a chunk of ice from the glass and dropped it down Berta's back.
>
> Now everybody was yelling. Carl was yelling because he couldn't find his keys. Berta was yelling because of the ice down her back. Fern was yelling because the others were making so much noise that she couldn't watch TV. And Herman was yelling because Carl was yelling at him about the keys.

1. Why was Carl yelling? _____

2. Where had Irma put the keys? _____

3. Why was Berta yelling? _____

4. What did Fern want to do? _____

5. Why was Herman yelling? _____

_____

Part 2

Write these words without endings.

1. opened   _____   5. pizzas   _____

2. removed   _____   6. worker   _____

3. placed   _____   7. hardly   _____

4. wearing   _____   8. slipped   _____

Details, suffixes

   Lesson 38   **75**

Part 3

A Chunk of Ice Down the Back

Irma had warned the others. But they didn't take her	10
warning. They yelled at her and told her that she had a lot of	24
nerve for talking to them that way.	31
Irma did not fight with them. She sat and ate her taco while	44
they yelled at her. Then she cleaned up the kitchen while they	56
went into the living room, and when they were watching TV,	67
she went downstairs.	70
She was pretty mad. At first she wanted to do the meanest	82
thing she could think of. But she sat and cooled off for a while.	96
Then she said, "I must think of a plan that is clever."	108
After thinking for a while, she said, "I've got it." She got a	121
pick and a hammer. She broke a chunk of paint from the pot of	135
invisible paint. She began to rub the paint on every part of her.	148
Then she slipped the invisible glasses on and went upstairs.	158
Irma was thinking, "They yell at me so much that they don't	170
have time to fight with each other. I will fix that."	181
She went to Carl's room. She felt in the pockets of Carl's	193
coat. She found his car keys. She carried the keys in to the living	207
room.	208

A Note to the Parent

Listen to the student read the passage. Count the number of words read in one minute and the number of errors.

Number of words read _____   Number of errors _____

We read the story _____ times.

(Parent's/Listener's) signature _____

Date _____

Reading fluency

Name _____

Part 1

Write the words.

1. what   + is   = _____

2. you   + are   = _____

3. should + not   = _____

4. that   + is   = _____

5. we   + will = _____

6. does   + not   = _____

7. we   + have = _____

8. I   + am   = _____

9. can   + not   = _____

10. you   + had   = _____

Part 2

Fill in the circle next to the word that completes the sentence. Write the word in the blank.

1. Irma will _____ him money to pay the dentist's bill.   ○ land   ○ lend

2. It was a _____ for her to get the paint off.   ○ bother   ○ brother

3. She fumbled around on the work _____ until she   ○ bench   ○ beach
   found the invisible glasses.

4. She left the room and _____ to see what would happen.   ○ wanted   ○ waited

Part 3

Write the compound words.

1. every + one   = _____

2. some   + times = _____

3. in   + side = _____

4. down   + stairs = _____

5. it   + self   = _____

6. through + out   = _____

Contractions, vocabulary/context clues, compound words

Name _____

Part 4

The Big Argument

Irma had done some things to start an argument between	10
her boarders. She had removed Carl's keys from his coat and	21
slipped them into Herman's pocket. She had taken a glass and	32
placed it next to Carl. Then she had taken a chunk of ice from	46
the glass and dropped it down Berta's back.	54
Now everybody was yelling. Carl was yelling because he	63
couldn't find his keys. Berta was yelling because of the ice down	75
her back. Fern was yelling because the others were making	85
so much noise that she couldn't watch TV. And Herman was	96
yelling because Carl was yelling at him about the keys.	106
All at once Herman stood up. "Come on," he said to Carl.	118
"If you think I've got your keys, look in my pockets. Come on."	131
"All right, I will," Carl said.	137
"No, you won't," Herman said. "Just keep your hands to	147
yourself. I'll show you what's in my pockets."	155
Herman took some coins from his front pocket. "There,"	164
he said. "Do those look like your keys?" Then he took some	176
folded money from another pocket. "Maybe you think that	185
these are yours, too?" Then Herman took the keys from his	196
back pocket. He held them up and said, "The next thing you	208
know, you'll be telling me that these are your keys."	218

A Note to the Parent

Listen to the student read the passage. Count the number of words read in one minute and the number of errors.

Number of words read _____ Number of errors _____

We read the story _____ times.

(Parent's/Listener's) signature _____

Date _____

Reading fluency

Lesson 40

Name _____

Part 1

Read the words in the box. Then fill in the blanks.

simmering	nice	brother	tacos	fish	smiled
arguing	stared	smiles	complain	spilled	slipped
tired	bother	cheese	yelled	pizza	cola
peace	started	complaining	late	scared	warned

Now Irma's boarders didn't _____ her. They didn't yell. They didn't

_____. They seemed to be tired of _____. In fact,

Herman was even _____ to her from time to time. One time she came

home with a _____. Carl _____ to say something about how

_____ she was, and Herman said, "Listen here. She works in that

_____ factory all day and still brings us dinner. So stop _____."

Irma _____ at Herman and said, "Well, thank you, Herman. That was a

very nice thing for you to say."

Part 2

Write the words without endings.

1. fumbles   _____

2. simmering   _____

3. slipped   _____

4. prices   _____

5. smiled   _____

6. scared   _____

7. whistled   _____

8. nearly   _____

Vocabulary/context clues, suffixes

Name _____

Part 3

Another Big Argument

After Irma had given the others a hand, they had been quiet	12
for a few days. After she made them argue among themselves,	23
they were quiet again. But on the third day after the argument,	35
Herman began to complain again. He was mad because he had	46
to go to the dentist. He complained about the dentist's bill for	58
his false tooth. He shouldn't have complained because Irma	67
loaned him the money to pay the dentist's bill.	76
Two days later, everybody was complaining again. They	84
complained because Irma came home with hamburgers.	91
"Hamburgers again?" they moaned. "Oh, I can't stand	99
hamburgers."	100
Irma said, "Remember what happened last time? If you're	109
mean to me, I'll be mean to you."	117
"Oh, be quiet, and let's eat," Herman said. His false tooth	128
was whiter than his other teeth.	134
"Okay," she remarked. "Just remember what I said."	142
Everybody yelled at Irma as they ate. So after dinner Irma	153
went down to her lab. She wasn't in the mood to rub invisible	166
paint all over her. She didn't mind rubbing the paint on so	178
much. But it was a bother to get the paint off. First she had to	193
rub herself with oil. Then she had to take a shower.	204

A Note to the Parent

Listen to the student read the passage. Count the number of words read in one minute and the number of errors.

Number of words read _____ Number of errors _____

We read the story _____ times.

(Parent's/Listener's) signature _____

Date _____

Reading fluency

Lesson 41

Name _____

Part 1

Fill in the circle next to the word that completes the sentence. Write the word in the blank.

1. Then one day, Irma made up her _____ to keep the paint. ○ mind ○ mine

2. From time to time, Berta would start to _____ about Irma. ○ grip ○ gripe

3. When this happened, Herman would say, "Stop _____." ○ gripping ○ griping

4. It's so nice and _____ in this room. ○ quiet ○ quite

Part 2

Write the two words that make up each word.

1. downstairs   =   _____   +   _____

2. yourself   =   _____   +   _____

3. billboard   =   _____   +   _____

4. everybody   =   _____   +   _____

5. outside   =   _____   +   _____

6. nothing   =   _____   +   _____

7. anyone   =   _____   +   _____

8. bedroom   =   _____   +   _____

Part 3

Write the words.

1. was   + not =   _____   3. I   + have =   _____

2. there   + is   =   _____   4. should + not =   _____

Vocabulary/context, compound words, contractions

Name _____

Part 4

Things Get Better

Irma didn't like the idea of paying for two more false teeth,	12
but she said to herself, "I think it's worth the price." One of	25
Herman's false teeth did not fit quite right. And when he said	37
words with an *s* in them, he whistled. He could say, "What are	50
we having for dinner?" without whistling. But when he said,	60
"I smell something simmering on the stove," he sounded like a	71
bird.	72
For two weeks after the last argument nobody yelled at	82
Irma. By now Herman had two new false teeth. Carl's nose was	94
smaller. And Fern's sore back was almost well.	102
For two weeks everybody seemed tired of arguing. But then	112
it started up again. Everybody began to pick on Irma. And	123
Irma warned them. She pointed her finger at them and said, "If	135
you give me a hard time, I will see to it that you get a hard time	152
right back."	154
They told her to shut up.	160
That night Irma put the invisible glasses on their cat and	171
let the cat walk through the living room. Berta passed out.	182
Herman saw the cat and spilled his glass of cola on Carl. Carl	195
did not see the cat.	200

A Note to the Parent

Listen to the student read the passage. Count the number of words read in one minute and the number of errors.

Number of words read _____   Number of errors _____

We read the story _____ times.

(Parent's/Listener's) signature _____

Date _____

Reading fluency

Lesson 42

Name _____

Part 1

Read the sentences in the box and answer the questions.

> When Old Salt had first moved into that little white house a year before, the girls and boys hadn't made fun of him. They listened to Old Salt tell about his days as a first officer on cargo ships. They heard him tell about the First World War and the Second World War. They listened to his tales about a chest of gold that had been taken from the SS *Foil* just before it had gone down in the South Pacific. The old man told the boys and girls that the *Foil* had sunk in 1918, while World War I was going on.

1. For how long had Old Salt lived in the house? _____

2. What job did he have on cargo ships? _____

3. What did he say was taken from the SS *Foil* before it sank? _____

4. What is the South Pacific? _____

5. What was going on in the year 1918? _____

Part 2

Write these words without endings.

1. retired _____   **6.** later _____

2. relatives _____   **7.** loved _____

3. mumbled _____   **8.** liking _____

4. really _____   **9.** certainly _____

5. worker _____   **10.** tales _____

Part 3

Write the words.

1. he   +   would   = _____   **3.** they   +   are   = _____

2. what   +   is   = _____   **4.** had   +   not   = _____

Details, suffixes, contractions

Part 4

Things Get Very Good

When Irma had begun working in her lab, she had hoped	11
that she would make a super hard paint. She had hoped that	23
she would become rich and powerful. But instead of inventing	33
a super hard paint, she had invented a paint that made things	45
invisible. And now she wasn't too sure about telling anybody	55
about her paint.	58
Here's how she saw it: If she told people about the paint,	70
she would make a lot of money. But who would want to use the	84
paint? Crooks would like to use it. They could rub the paint	96
on themselves and rob banks. And nobody would be safe if	107
that paint got on the market. You wouldn't be able to tell when	120
somebody was in the room with you.	127
When you walked down the street at night, you wouldn't	137
know when an invisible hand might reach out and grab you.	148
The crooks would love the invisible paint, but the cops would	159
hate it. Spies would love it. Bankers would hate it. Con men	171
would love it. People with cash in their pockets would hate it.	183
Irma did a lot of thinking about her paint. From time to	195
time she told herself, "I don't care how people use this paint."	207

A Note to the Parent Listen to the student read the passage. Count the number of words read in one minute and the number of errors.

Number of words read _____ Number of errors _____

We read the story _____ times.

(Parent's/Listener's) signature _____

Date _____

Reading fluency

Lesson 43

Name _____

Part 1

Write the words. Item 1 is done for you.

1. like + ing = _____liking_____

2. nose + ing = _____

3. take + en = _____

4. try + ing = _____

5. decide + ed = _____

6. snap + ed = _____

7. young + er = _____

8. store + ed = _____

9. magnify + ing = _____

10. kid + ing = _____

Part 2

Write the two words that make up each compound word.

1. outside = _____ + _____

2. everybody = _____ + _____

3. matchbox = _____ + _____

4. sometime = _____ + _____

5. without = _____ + _____

6. downstairs = _____ + _____

7. herself = _____ + _____

8. classroom = _____ + _____

Part 3

Write the words. Item 1 is done for you.

1. will + not = _____won't_____

2. do + not = _____

3. she + is = _____

4. were + not = _____

5. you + have = _____

6. we + will = _____

Suffixes, compound words, contractions

Part 4

Old Salt, the Retired Sailor

They called him Old Salt, and they liked to make fun of	12
him. Old Salt was a retired sailor. They didn't hate him. They	24
didn't really think that they were being mean to him. They just	36
liked to make him mad. So when they went past his house on	49
their way to school, they would call to him, "Hey, Old Salt.	61
Have you found your ship yet? Hey—Salt! Let's go hunting for	73
treasures."	74
"Be on your way," Old Salt would holler from his window.	85
"What do you know about hidden treasures?"	92
"Come on, Salt," the kids would yell. "Let's go hunting for	103
treasures."	104
"Be on your way," Salt would yell. Then he'd mumble to	115
himself, and the kids would laugh.	121
When Old Salt had first moved into that little white house	132
a year before, the girls and boys hadn't made fun of him. They	145
listened to Old Salt tell about his days as a first officer on cargo	159
ships. They heard him tell about the Second World War. They	170
listened to his tales about a chest of gold that had been taken	183
from the SS *Foil* just before it had gone down in the South	197
Pacific.	198

A Note to the Parent

Listen to the student read the passage. Count the number of words read in one minute and the number of errors.

Number of words read _____   Number of errors _____

We read the story _____ times.

(Parent's/Listener's) signature _____

Date _____

Reading fluency

Name _____

Part 1

Read the words in the box. Then fill in the blanks.

unfold	thousand	hundreds	parted	specks	shipped
shaped	painted	dotted	decide	sense	crack
fumbled	meal	start	maps	numbers	spoil
spell	pointed	chance	knock	close	find

Old Salt said, "If only we could _____ out where this island is, we would be

off to a good _____. But there must be a _____ little islands in the

South Pacific. This could be any one of them. Look for yourself."

Salt _____ to a big wall map of the South Pacific. It was _____

with little islands. Most of them looked like _____. You couldn't tell from the map

if they were _____ like an *S*, like a *C*, or like an *I*. All of them looked like little dots.

Salt said, "I think those _____ at the top of the map tell where the island is.

But I haven't been able to _____ the code."

Part 2

Write the words.

1. was + not = _____
2. will + not = _____
3. here + is = _____

4. that + is = _____
5. does + not = _____
6. we + are = _____

Part 3

1. Write the word **decide.** Make a line over **ci.**   _____

2. Write the word **farther.** Make a line over **ar.**   _____

3. Write the word **loudly.** Make a line under **ou.**   _____

Vocabulary/context, contractions, word parts

Name _____

Part 4

The Captain's Chest

A truck was parked in front of Old Salt's house. Salt was	12
holding the door open for the two workers who were carrying a	24
big trunk into the house. Tony had asked if they could look at	37
the stuff in the trunk.	42
Salt stared at Tony. He was trying to see if Tony was going	55
to make fun of him.	60
Tony said, "I'm not kidding, Salt. I'd really like to see what's	72
in it."	74
Salt turned away. Without looking at Tony, he said, "Come	84
around. Come around sometime, and we'll see what we'll see."	94
Rosa yelled, "Yeah, Salt. Maybe it's a treasure."	102
"Knock it off," Tony said. "Don't make fun of him all the	114
time. That stuff gets old after a while."	122
After school Tony said to Rosa, "Hey, let's go over to Old	134
Salt's place and see what's in that trunk."	142
Rosa shook her head. "No, I don't think so." Then she	153
shrugged. "Well, why not? Let's go."	159
So they went to Old Salt's place. They knocked on the door.	171
They could hear Salt walking to the door. He walked with a	183
limp. He opened the door. He stared at them.	192
"Come to make fun of my captain, have you?"	201

A Note to the Parent

Listen to the student read the passage. Count the number of words read in one minute and the number of errors.

Number of words read _____   Number of errors _____

We read the story _____ times.

(Parent's/Listener's) signature _____

Date _____

Reading fluency

Lesson 45

Name _____

Part 1

Match the words and complete them.

volcano		oi
poison		sure
sprang		or
treasure		cano
thorns		rang

peace		er
speck		ch
thousands		ea
bunch		ck
numbers		ou

Part 2

Write the words.

1. make + ing = _____

2. store + ed = _____

3. solve + ed = _____

4. hike + ing = _____

5. pace + s = _____

6. peer + ed = _____

7. set + ing = _____

8. pass + ed = _____

9. large + er = _____

10. grip + ed = _____

Part 3

Write the two words that make up each word.

1. won't = _____ + _____

2. where's = _____ + _____

3. couldn't = _____ + _____

4. I've = _____ + _____

5. you're = _____ + _____

6. she'll = _____ + _____

Word match, suffixes, contractions

Part 4

Cracking the Code

Tony and Rosa didn't see Salt for over a week. Salt was	12
inside working on the code. Nine days after the trunk had	23
arrived at Salt's house, Tony saw Salt outside. It was a warm	35
day. It had just rained, and puddles of water were on the	47
ground. Salt was sitting on his front steps.	55
"Hello," Tony said. "How are you coming with the code on	66
the *Foil* map?"	69
Salt shook his head. "Ah," he said, "that sure is a hard one.	82
Worked day and night, I have. And still I can't make heads nor	95
tails out of it. I think it is beyond me."	105
"Maybe you need some help," Tony said. "What if I helped	116
you work on the code?"	121
Salt shook his head. "I don't know about that." His eyes	132
looked at Tony. Then they looked down. "It might be that you	144
could help."	146
"I'm ready," Tony said. "Let's take a look at that map."	157
Just then Rosa came down the street on her bike. She	168
stopped and said, "Am I missing out on something?"	177
"Yeah," Tony said. "We're going to work on the code. Salt	188
hasn't broken it yet."	192

A Note to the Parent

Listen to the student read the passage. Count the number of words read in one minute and the number of errors.

Number of words read _____   Number of errors _____

We read the story _____ times.

(Parent's/Listener's) signature _____

Date _____

Reading fluency

Name _____

Part 1

Read the sentences in the box and answer the questions.

> "How much is the gold worth?" Tony asked.
>
> "That's not a thing to be talking about," Salt said sharply. He looked boiling mad. "Don't talk about gold," he said.
>
> "I'm sorry, Salt," Tony said. "Are you going to see about getting a ship?"
>
> Salt shook his head, "Don't talk about that," he said. "Just go off to school and think about something else."
>
> So Tony went to school. It seemed like a long day. It seemed as if the three o'clock bell would never ring. But at last it did, and Tony ran all the way to Salt's house. Now he would find out about the ship.

1. What two things did Old Salt tell Tony not to talk about? _____

2. What did Salt tell Tony to do instead? _____

_____

3. Why did the school day seem so long to Tony? _____

_____

4. What did Tony hope to find out about after school? _____

Part 2

Write these words without endings.

1. tales   _____   6. boiling   _____

2. slowly   _____   7. stopped   _____

3. getting   _____   8. quickly   _____

4. having   _____   9. places   _____

5. talked   _____   10. sharper   _____

Details, suffixes

Name _____

Part 3

The Code Is Broken

Tony and Rosa and Old Salt broke part of the map's code.	12
The numbers on the top of the map said: "SS *Foil,* Rose	25
Island."	26
"Rose Island," Old Salt said. He sprang from his chair and	37
darted to the map. "It's right around here," he said. He pointed	49
to three or four places on the map. Then he asked, "Where's my	62
glass? How can I read this map without my glass?"	72
Rosa handed him the big magnifying glass. "Here it is," Salt	83
said, and pointed to one of the little dots between two larger	95
dots. "Rose Island," he said. "I remember it well. Flowers, trees,	106
and black-sand beaches. The water is filled with poison coral. If	117
you step on it, you're dead."	123
"Did you say the sand on the beach is black?" Rosa asked.	135
"As black as night," Old Salt said.	142
"I've never seen black sand," Tony said.	149
"You see," Salt said, "at one time—thousands and	158
thousands of years ago—Rose Island was a volcano sticking	168
out of the sea. The waves have worn the island down over the	181
years. The rock from the volcano is black, so the sand on the	194
beach is black."	197
"Wow!" Tony said. "Why do they call it Rose Island?"	207

A Note to the Parent

Listen to the student read the passage. Count the number of words read in one minute and the number of errors.

Number of words read _____ Number of errors _____

We read the story _____ times.

(Parent's/Listener's) signature _____

Date _____

Reading fluency

Lesson 47

Name _____

Part 1
Read the sentences in the box and answer the questions.

> Rosa and Tony bent over the table. Salt talked very softly. He told them that a vacation ship was leaving for the South Pacific in three weeks. Salt said that he could get a job on that ship. The ship would go as far as Wake Island. From that point, Salt would have to rent a small boat and travel 300 miles to Rose Island.

1. What kind of ship was leaving for the South Pacific? _____

2. When would the ship leave? _____

3. How did Salt plan to pay for the trip? _____

4. Where is Wake Island? _____

5. How did Salt plan to get from Wake Island to Rose Island? _____

_____

6. How far is it from Wake Island to Rose Island? _____

Part 2
Write the words.

1. trap   + ed = _____   4. broke   + en = _____

2. puddle + s   = _____   5. bite   + ing = _____

3. let   + ing = _____   6. sharp   + ly = _____

Part 3
Write the two words that make up each word.

1. won't   = _____   + _____

2. there's = _____   + _____

3. you'll   = _____   + _____

4. I'm   = _____   + _____

5. they're = _____   + _____

6. can't   = _____   + _____

Details, suffixes, contractions

Part 4

Dreams of Gold

Now Tony and Rosa and Old Salt had broken the whole	11
code. Numbers stood for letters, and letters stood for numbers.	21
Z-16 was a code for twenty-six paces.	29
"Not a word of this to anybody," Old Salt said when Rosa	41
and Tony were leaving his house. "Tonight we cracked the code.	52
Tomorrow I'll see about getting on a ship to Rose Island."	63
Rosa and Tony walked slowly down the street. They talked	73
for a while in front of their house. Then they went inside. Tony	86
went to his bedroom and sat on his bed. He sat for a long time,	101
thinking about the map and treasure. It was funny, thinking	111
about a real treasure.	115
Tony felt like an adult and a child at the same time. He felt	129
like an adult because treasure hunting is something that adults	139
do. On the other hand, he felt like a child because he wanted to	153
tell everybody about the treasure. He wanted to tell his mom	164
and his dad, his little brother, and his dog. He wanted to tell his	178
friends at school. He wanted to tell everybody.	186
Think of it—Tony Rizzo finding a treasure! Was all of this	198
real, or was Tony just having a dream?	206

A Note to the Parent

Listen to the student read the passage. Count the number of words read in one minute and the number of errors.

Number of words read _____ Number of errors _____

We read the story _____ times.

(Parent's/Listener's) signature _____

Date _____

Reading fluency

Lesson 48

Name _____

Part 1

Read the words in the box. Then fill in the blanks.

placed	four	worked	kidding	week	grime
weak	stopped	fished	mess	cook	button
three	sailor	blazing	pointed	crime	painted
passed	boiler	streaked	showed	rammed	chunks

For _____ hours Tony _____ clinkers from the furnace. He

had a long, _____ rod. He _____ the rod into the clinkers. Then

he lifted them from the furnace.

After four hours had _____, a _____ came to Tony and said,

"Okay, you're off for four hours." Tony was a _____. He was covered with grit

and _____. His face was _____ with sweat. His hands were sore.

His legs were _____.

Part 2
Write the words.

1. late   + er   = _____

2. change + ed   = _____

3. pat   + ed   = _____

4. pile   + ing = _____

5. carry   + ing = _____

6. open   + ed   = _____

7. quick   + ly   = _____

8. hire   + ed   = _____

Part 3
Write the words.

1. It + is   = _____

2. he + would = _____

3. we + have = _____

4. she + has   = _____

Vocabulary/context, suffixes, contractions

Part 4

Name _____

How to Get to Wake Island

Tony could hardly wait to get to Salt's house and meet with	12
Salt and Rosa. There was a lot to talk about. All day in school	26
Tony had thought about the treasure.	32
When Tony got to Salt's house, Rosa was already there.	42
And Salt was boiling mad. Salt was saying, "You've got to stop	54
talking about gold." Then his voice became soft. "Somebody	63
will steal the map if you don't stop talking about it."	74
Tony said, "Well, I just can't stop thinking about it."	84
"Think all you want," Salt said. "But when you feel like	95
talking about it, just bite your lip."	102
"Okay," Tony said.	105
Salt led them to the upstairs room. Then they sat around	116
the table. Salt said, "From now on, we will write in code. If you	130
want to know something, write it in code."	138
"That's a good idea," Rosa said. "If we do that, nobody will	150
know what we're saying."	154
"Right," Salt said. "Now let me tell you what I found out	166
about the ship."	169
Rosa and Tony bent over the table. Salt talked very softly.	180
He told them that a vacation ship was leaving for the South	192
Pacific in three weeks. Salt said that he could get a job on that	206
ship.	207

A Note to the Parent

Listen to the student read the passage. Count the number of words read in one minute and the number of errors.

Number of words read _____ Number of errors _____

We read the story _____ times.

(Parent's/Listener's) signature _____

Date _____

Reading fluency

Name _____

Part 1

Read the sentences in the box and answer the questions.

> The ship had made five stops. This was the last one. It would stay at Wake Island for three days. Then it would go back home. But Tony, Rosa, and Salt would not be on it. They would be in a small boat on their way to Rose Island.
>
> That night Tony, Rosa, and Salt were standing on the dock again, talking to a woman who had small boats for rent. The night air was sweet with the smell of wild flowers. And the air was hot and wet.
>
> Salt was saying to the woman at the dock. "We need a boat that can go six hundred miles out to sea."

1. For how long would the vacation ship stay at Wake Island? _____

2. When the ship went back home, where would Salt, Rosa, and Tony be? _____

_____

3. Why did they meet with the woman on the dock? _____

_____

4. What made the air smell sweet? _____

5. How did the air feel? _____

6. What kind of boat did Salt say they needed? _____

_____

7. How far is it from Wake Island to Rose Island? _____

Part 2

Write the words.

1. gripe + ing = _____   **6.** large + er = _____

2. hard + ly = _____   **7.** move + ed = _____

3. believe + ed = _____   **8.** slap + ing = _____

4. wave + ing = _____   **9.** final + ly = _____

5. small + er = _____   **10.** like + ing = _____

Details, inferences, endings

Part 3

On the Ship

Tony and Rosa tried and tried to make their mother and	11
dad let them go on the trip to the South Pacific. Then it	24
happened. Somehow Rosa and Tony talked their parents into it.	34
Maybe they wore their parents down. Maybe their parents just	44
got tired of saying, "No." But it happened.	52
Their mother talked to their father. They all talked to Old	63
Salt. Salt told their parents that he would look out for Tony	75
and Rosa. Their parents talked some more. Then, after a week	86
of talking and talking, the kids' mother and father said, "Well,	97
all right. You can go."	102
Tony jumped up in the air. He yelled. Rosa ran around the	114
kitchen. Then Tony and Rosa kissed their mother and ran over	125
to Salt's house.	128
And somehow the kids got jobs on the ship. Rosa got a job	141
waiting tables. Tony got a job in the boiler room. The man who	154
hired them told Tony, "This is a hard job, and I don't know if	168
you can do it. But I'll give you a chance."	178
Everything was set. Salt got the tools they would need to	189
dig up the chest. He had a coil of thick rope.	200

A Note to the Parent

Listen to the student read the passage. Count the number of words read in one minute and the number of errors.

Number of words read _____ Number of errors _____

We read the story _____ times.

(Parent's/Listener's) signature _____

Date _____

Reading fluency

Name _____

Part 1

Read the words in the box. Then fill in the blanks.

birds	place	pop	green	feet	string
beach	swim	distance	sheet	gallon	surface
wash	dock	melt	volcano	yellow	bring
shovels	ring	pile	bugs	wild	claws

The sky in the east was starting to turn _____. The sea was as smooth as

a _____ of glass. Every now and then a little fish would _____

out of the water and leave a _____ that moved slowly and seemed to

_____ into the smooth _____ of the water. The vacation ship

was dark, except for the _____ of lights on the top deck. Little birds were

walking on the _____. So were big crabs with _____ that could

cut off your finger. The _____ seemed to be everywhere.

Part 2

Write the compound words.

1. every + where = _____

2. speed + boat = _____

3. flash + light = _____

4. out + fit = _____

5. after + noon = _____

6. some + how = _____

7. pass + port = _____

8. your + self = _____

9. when + ever = _____

10. any + thing = _____

Vocabulary/context, compound words

Part 3

Wake Island

Salt, Tony, and Rosa had jobs on the big, old vacation ship,	12
and it was going to the South Pacific. At first Tony was mad	25
because his job was so hard. Rosa and Salt had easy jobs. But	38
by the time the ship reached Wake Island, Tony was beginning	49
to think that he had the best deal of the three. He toiled harder	63
than the others, but his job made him very strong. His hands	75
became strong from gripping that clinker rod. His back and legs	86
were strong. When the ship docked at Wake Island, Tony was in	98
the best shape he'd ever been in.	105
The sun was boiling hot that day. Rosa, Tony, and Salt	116
stood on the lower deck of the ship and looked at Wake Island.	129
The ship's horn was going, "Toot, toot, toot." Other ships	139
and small boats were tooting back. The people on deck were	150
waving and shouting. The people on the dock were waving and	161
shouting.	162
As Tony stood there, he could hardly believe what was	172
happening. His home and his school seemed very far away. He	183
had been on the ship for thirty-two days.	191
The ship had made five stops. This was the last one.	202

A Note to the Parent

Listen to the student read the passage. Count the number of words read in one minute and the number of errors.

Number of words read _____ Number of errors _____

We read the story _____ times.

(Parent's/Listener's) signature _____

Date _____

Reading fluency

Lesson 51

Name _____

Part 1

Read the sentences in the box and answer the questions.

> The island didn't look the way Tony had thought it would. It looked much bigger than he had thought. And the cliffs were much higher than he had thought.
> At last the boat came to the place where there were no cliffs. There was a little cove. The water in the cove was clear and very green. Tony could see fish swimming under the surface of the water. The boat slid up on the black-sand beach. Salt cut the engine, and everything was calm, except for the hooting of birds.

1. Name two ways that the island looked different than Tony thought it would look.

_____

2. Salt, Tony, and Rosa found a place to land the boat where there were no cliffs. What place was that? _____

3. What was the water like in the cove? _____

4. What kind of beach did they land on? _____

5. After Salt turned off the motor, what was the only sound they could hear?

_____

Part 2

Write the words.

1. start + er = _____
2. slap + ed = _____
3. snore + ed = _____
4. pile + ing = _____
5. spray + ed = _____

6. pace + ing = _____
7. bounce + ed = _____
8. shake + ing = _____
9. speckle + ed = _____
10. bob + ing = _____

Part 3

Write the words.

1. you + had = _____
2. we + have = _____

3. do + not = _____
4. he + has = _____

Details/inferences, suffixes, contractions

Lesson 51 **101**

Part 4

The Trip to Rose Island

The sky in the east was starting to turn yellow. The sea was	13
as smooth as a sheet of glass. Every now and then a little fish	27
would pop out of the water and leave a ring that moved slowly	40
and seemed to melt into the smooth surface of the water. The	52
vacation ship was dark, except for a string of lights on the top	65
deck. Little birds were walking on the beach. So were big crabs	77
with claws that could cut off your finger. The bugs seemed to be	90
everywhere. The boat was almost packed.	96
"Where are the shovels?" asked Rosa.	102
"They're packed," Salt said.	106
"What about food and water?" Tony asked.	113
"We have plenty," Salt said.	118
Rosa said, "That means we're ready to go."	126
Tony said, "What about gas?"	131
"We have plenty of that, too," Salt said.	139
Tony jumped into the boat. It didn't rock much, but it sent	151
out three waves. The waves moved across the still water. Then	162
Rosa got into the boat. And then Salt started the motor.	173
"Rrrrr-rrr-rrrr," went the starter. Then, "Chu-cug, chu-cug,"	180
went the motor. The boat started to move. The three of them	192
were going out into the still sea, all alone.	201

A Note to the Parent

Listen to the student read the passage. Count the number of words read in one minute and the number of errors.

Number of words read _____ Number of errors _____

We read the story _____ times.

(Parent's/Listener's) signature _____

Date _____

Reading fluency

Part 1

Read the words in the box. Then fill in the blanks.

stream	stopped	back	foot	dense	mapped
twisted	paced	top	letter	mopped	spray
arrow	left	filtered	edge	lucky	soaked
tied	slope	squinted	pointed	turned	ferns

They stopped at the _____ of a stream. They jumped across the stream,

turned more toward the west, and _____ off another twenty-six paces. They

stopped at the edge of the very steep _____.

"This must have been the _____ of the volcano," Salt said. "So far we've

been _____. There has been a landmark for everything _____ on

the map."

Now Salt and the others _____ south. The map said *W-16*. So Salt stepped

off twenty-three paces and _____ . There was no landmark.

Salt _____ the sweat from his face. He _____ and looked

through the underbrush. "No landmark," he said. "But let's go on."

Part 2

Write the two words that make up each compound word.

1. underbrush = _____ + _____

2. landmarks = _____ + _____

3. sunlight = _____ + _____

4. southwest = _____ + _____

Part 3

Write the words.

1. pace + ed = _____   **4.** holler + ed = _____

2. slight + ly = _____   **5.** excited + ed = _____

3. rot + ing = _____   **6.** smile + ing = _____

Vocabulary/context, compound words, suffixes

Lesson 52

Part 4

Rose Island at Last

Tony steered the boat most of the night. When the sky	11
began to grow light, the sea became choppy again. Each time	22
the front of the boat went through a wave, water sprayed into	34
the air. Some of it landed in the boat.	43
"Hey," Rosa said, "turn the boat so that it doesn't make so	55
much spray."	57
Old Salt jumped up from the back of the boat. "You'd have	69
Tony do that?" he yelled. "You'd have him miss Rose Island	80
after we've come all this way?"	86
"No," Rosa said. "I'm just getting tired of getting wet."	96
Salt smiled. A wave with a curl of white water slapped the	108
front of the boat. Rosa was soaked. Salt was soaked, but he	120
kept on smiling. Then he said, "There she be. There be Rose	132
Island."	133
Tony tried to stand up. But the boat was bobbing so much	145
that it knocked Tony down.	150
"We're there," Salt said. "We'll be on dry land before you	161
know it."	163
Two hours later, the boat was next to the island. They	174
hadn't landed yet, but they were near the cove on the north end	187
of the island. Tony watched the waves dash against the high	198
cliffs of the island.	202

A Note to the Parent

Listen to the student read the passage. Count the number of words read in one minute and the number of errors.

Number of words read _____ Number of errors _____

We read the story _____ times.

(Parent's/Listener's) signature _____

Date _____

Reading fluency

Lesson 53

Name _____

Part 1

Write **1, 2, 3,** or **4** in front of each sentence to show when these things happened in the story. Then write the sentences in the blanks.

_____ Salt uncoiled a rope and tied one end of it around the handle of the knife.

_____ Tony found a knife handle in the pile of rocks.

_____ Suddenly, a huge pile of rocks came sliding down the side of the volcano.

_____ Salt tugged and tugged until the knife came out of the ground.

1. _____

_____

2. _____

_____

3. _____

_____

4. _____

_____

Part 2

Write the words.

1. he   +   had   = _____

2. it   +   is   = _____

3. did   +   not   = _____

4. we   +   are   = _____

5. where   +   is   = _____

6. will   +   not   = _____

7. you   +   will   = _____

8. I   +   am   = _____

Part 3

Write the words.

1. rumble + ing = _____

2. rust   + y   = _____

3. rattle   + ing = _____

4. tug   + ed   = _____

5. bite   + ing = _____

6. cool   + er   = _____

Sequence, contractions, suffixes

Name _____

Part 4

More Landmarks

Everything was green inside the jungle. Even the light was	10
green. Tony's white shirt looked green. No sunlight got through	20
the dense trees. Only a green glow filtered down to the floor of	33
the jungle.	35
Salt was leading the way. Tony followed. Then came Rosa.	45
After they reached the huge, moss-covered rock, they turned	54
slightly to the south and paced off another twenty-six paces.	64
They stopped at the edge of the stream. They jumped across	75
the stream, turned more toward the west, and paced off	85
another twenty-six paces. They stopped at the edge of a very	96
steep slope.	98
"This must be the foot of the volcano," Salt said. "So far	110
we've been lucky. There has been a landmark for every arrow	121
on the map."	124
Now Salt and the others turned south. The map said *W-16*.	136
So Salt stepped off twenty-three paces and stopped. There was	146
no landmark.	148
Salt mopped the sweat from his face. He squinted and	158
looked through the underbrush. "No landmark," he said. "But	167
let's go on. We know that we were going right when we got to	181
the foot of the volcano."	186
The next arrow on the map was pointing due west. The map	198
said *X-16*. "Twenty-four paces," Salt said and began to step	209
them off.	211

▶ A Note to the Parent

Listen to the student read the passage. Count the number of words read in one minute and the number of errors.

Number of words read _____ Number of errors _____

We read the story _____ times.

(Parent's/Listener's) signature _____

Date _____

Reading fluency

Name _____

Part 1 Read the words in the box. Then fill in the blanks.

knife	pushed	peered	rusty	bent	patted
find	bobbed	volcano	handle	paced	shovel
piles	traps	tugged	ledge	chain	bands
soil	scrambled	cove	corner	rocks	lock

Tony and Rosa _____ up the side of the _____. Tony remembered to bring

his _____. When they reached the _____, they saw Salt _____ over.

Without looking up, Salt said, "They put the treasure under the _____.

I don't see any more _____. Let's dig down and see what we

_____." Salt _____ the shovel into the ground. "Clink." He

tossed the dirt aside. And there it was, the _____ of the chest.

Part 2 Write the two words that make up each compound word.

1. breakfast = _____ + _____

2. something = _____ + _____

3. afternoon = _____ + _____

4. nothing = _____ + _____

5. maybe = _____ + _____

6. sunlight = _____ + _____

7. landslide = _____ + _____

8. whenever = _____ + _____

9. daytime = _____ + _____

Part 3 Write the words.

1. here + is = _____   3. you + have = _____

2. is + not = _____   4. were + not = _____

Vocabulary/context, contractions, word parts

Name _____

Part 4

Digging for Gold

Tony's hands were sore. His back was sore. So were his legs.	12
He was beginning to realize that Salt had been right when he'd	24
said that the real work was just beginning. For the past three	36
hours, Tony had hauled rocks from the pile. At first the pile had	49
been about six feet high. Now it was only about one foot high.	62
Tony bent down and grabbed another rock. When he picked	72
it up, he saw something below it. "Hey, Rosa," he said. "What's	84
that?"	85
Rosa tossed a rock into the underbrush. Then she wiped the	96
sweat from her eyes. She bent down and looked where Tony was	108
pointing. "It looks like a knife handle," Rosa said. "I'll pull it	120
out."	121
Rosa was about to grab the handle when Salt tackled her.	132
"No," Salt yelled. Salt and Rosa tumbled over the rock pile.	143
Then Salt sat up and said, "Don't touch it. It may be a trap."	157
"What do you mean?" Rosa asked. Rosa was rubbing her	167
arm.	168
Salt said, "If you had a treasure in the ground, would you	180
leave it without some kind of protection?"	187
"I don't know," Rosa said.	192
"Well, the people who put this treasure in the ground	202
wouldn't do that," Salt said.	207

A Note to the Parent

Listen to the student read the passage. Count the number of words read in one minute and the number of errors.

Number of words read _____ Number of errors _____

We read the story _____ times.

(Parent's/Listener's) signature _____

Date _____

Reading fluency

Lesson 55

Name _____

Part 1
Read the sentences in the box and answer the questions.

> The treasure didn't look the way Tony had thought that it would. He had thought that he would see heaps of shiny coins and gold crowns. He had thought that he would see huge red gems that sparkled and gold drinking cups. But he saw heaps of black coins. Some of them were covered with green mold. Some of them had specks of white on them, but most of them were black.
>
> There were three or four bugs in the chest, too. They scrambled down between the coins when the chest was opened.

1. Name three things that Tony thought he would see in the treasure chest.

   _____

2. What did he see instead? _____

3. What were some coins covered with? _____

4. What happened to the bugs in the chest? _____

   _____

Part 2
Write the words.

1. strange + er = _____
2. have   + ing = _____
3. taste   + ed = _____
4. sudden + ly = _____
5. stop   + ing = _____

6. uncover + ed = _____
7. sparkle + ed = _____
8. dance   + ing = _____
9. mop   + ed = _____
10. stare   + ing = _____

Part 3
Write the two words that make up each word.

1. shouldn't = _____ + _____

2. that's   = _____ + _____

3. I'll   = _____ + _____

4. we've   = _____ + _____

Details, suffixes, contractions

Name _____

Part 4

Where Is the Treasure Chest?

When Tony woke up, he smelled smoke. He looked around.	10
There was Salt cooking something over a fire. "What are we	21
having for breakfast?" Tony asked.	26
"It's a fine breakfast you'll have," Salt said. "Bananas and	36
coffee."	37
"Oh," Tony said. He wasn't very hungry for any more	47
bananas. He could still taste the bananas he'd eaten yesterday	57
and the day before. But bananas were better than nothing. So	68
Tony ate three bananas and tried to drink some of the coffee	80
Salt fixed. That coffee was so bitter that Tony couldn't drink	91
more than a few swallows.	96
But there was one good thing about the coffee. After you	107
drank some of it, you couldn't taste bananas any more. All you	119
could taste was coffee. And you could taste coffee all morning.	130
The taste hadn't left Tony's mouth by the time they reached	141
the foot of the volcano. It hadn't gone away when Tony and	153
Rosa started to work on the pile of rocks again. It hadn't even	166
gone away when it was time to stop for lunch and eat more	179
bananas. By the early afternoon all of the rocks had been	190
removed from the pile.	194
Salt pointed to the bare ground.	200

A Note to the Parent

Listen to the student read the passage. Count the number of words read in one minute and the number of errors.

Number of words read _____ Number of errors _____

We read the story _____ times.

(Parent's/Listener's) signature _____

Date _____

Reading fluency

Part 1
Write **1, 2, 3,** or **4** in front of each sentence to show when these things happened in the story. Then write the sentences in the blanks.

_____ Rosa, Tony, and Salt made eight trips to drag the sacks of gold down to the boat.

_____ Salt said they would get the treasure home if the sea wanted them to take it home.

_____ They figured out that 24 sacks of gold would be worth over seven million dollars.

_____ Salt, Tony, and Rosa put pretty stones in the sacks to hide the gold.

1. _____

_____

2. _____

_____

3. _____

_____

4. _____

_____

Part 2
Read the paragraphs and answer the questions.

"Don't talk that way," Tony said. "We've got the gold, and we're going to get it home. Right, Rosa?"

"Right," Rosa said. "If we have to swim home with those sacks, we'll get them home. Right, Salt?"

Salt smiled. "Yes. We'll get it home if the sea wants us to take it home. And I hope that the sea does just that. But remember, our boat is going to ride low in the water. There will be nearly 2,000 pounds of weight in the front of the boat. A good squall could send our treasure to the bottom of the ocean. Let's just hope that the sea is calm and that no squalls come up."

1. What was in the front of the boat? _____

_____

2. Why would the boat ride low in the water? _____

3. What could happen if a squall came up? _____

_____

Sequence, details/inferences

Part 3

Gold, Gold, Gold

Salt, Rosa, and Tony had found the chest that had been	11
buried on Rose Island. Salt reached inside a hole in the chest	23
and pulled out a gold coin.	29
The top of the chest was uncovered. A large, rusty lock	40
hung from the chest lid. Salt took his shovel and swung it hard.	53
He hit the lock. Bits of rust flew into the air. The lock swung	67
back and forth. Again Salt swung at the lock, and again bits	79
of rust flew into the air. On the third swing, the lock fell to the	94
ground in two pieces.	98
Salt wedged the scoop of his shovel under the lid of the	110
chest and pushed down. Slowly the lid began to move. Rosa and	122
Tony grabbed the lid and pulled up. The lid opened. For a long	135
moment, they stared into the chest. Nobody said a thing.	145
Tony looked into the chest, and he felt very strange. He	156
could hear himself breathing. In the distance were sounds of	166
jungle birds. His eyes were fixed on what he saw inside the	178
chest. It didn't look the way he had thought it would.	189
Tony had thought that he would see heaps of shiny coins	200
and gold crowns.	203

A Note to the Parent

Listen to the student read the passage. Count the number of words read in one minute and the number of errors.

Number of words read _____ Number of errors _____

We read the story _____ times.

(Parent's/Listener's) signature _____

Date _____

Reading fluency

Name _____

Part 1 Write **1, 2, 3,** or **4** in front of each sentence to show when these things happened in the story. Then write the sentences in the blanks.

_____ The bottom of the boat had nearly a foot of water in it.

_____ Within an hour, a stiff wind began to blow.

_____ Before long, the waves were rolling and pounding into the side of the boat.

_____ The air was foggy the next morning, and the sea was still very calm.

1. _____

_____

2. _____

_____

3. _____

_____

4. _____

Part 2 Read the words in the box. Then fill in the blanks.

side	hounding	boiling	rocking	stand	sink
sliding	size	lifting	sound	couple	bottom
setting	mass	limping	course	darker	foggy
gusts	foaming	floated	smell	head	scrambled

Before long, the waves were rolling and _____ and pounding into the side

of the boat. The fog was _____ now, and Tony could see that the ocean was a

_____ of white, _____ waves. The boat was _____

from side to side as the waves pounded against it. The _____ of the waves was

very loud.

Salt said, "We're going to have to change _____. Unless we

_____ into the wind, we'll _____. Those waves will soon be

coming over the _____ of the boat."

Sequence, vocabulary/context

Part 3

Loading the Boat

Rosa, Tony, and Salt were dragging bags of gold back to	11
the boat. Dragging the sacks through the jungle was not easy.	22
The sacks would drop into little holes. They would catch on the	34
underbrush. At one time Tony thought that it would be easier	45
to lift his sack and carry it. So he carried it for about twenty	59
feet. Then he decided that it would be much easier to drag the	72
sack.	73
Soon Salt and the others were standing at the rim of the	85
hill that led down to the shore. Salt tied the three pieces of rope	99
together. Then he began to let the sacks slide down the side of	112
the hill.	114
Rosa and Tony scrambled down the hill and held on to the	126
sacks. Then they carried the sacks to the boat.	135
Salt stood up and mopped the sweat from his face. "Look	146
around for some pretty stones," he said. "We'll put them in the	158
sacks. Then if anybody looks into any of the sacks, the person	170
will see stones, not gold."	175
"Good idea," Rosa said.	179
So Rosa and Tony went rock hunting. They found some	189
pretty red stones and some that had streaks of white and yellow	201
in them.	203

A Note to the Parent

Listen to the student read the passage. Count the number of words read in one minute and the number of errors.

Number of words read _____ Number of errors _____

We read the story _____ times.

(Parent's/Listener's) signature _____

Date _____

Reading fluency

Name _____

Part 1

Read the sentences in the box and answer the questions.

> Tony liked to think about the things that he could do with two million dollars. But every time he began to feel good about the gold, he remembered what Salt had said and became a little worried about the sea. Salt had said they wouldn't reach Wake Island until just before morning. They would still be in the boat all afternoon, all evening, and almost all of the night. That was a lot of time. And the sea could change quickly.
>
> Tony opened his eyes and looked around. Rosa was eating a banana. The sun was very hot.

1. What happened to Tony every time he began to feel good about the gold?

_____

_____   _____

2. When would they reach Wake Island? _____

3. How much longer would they be in the boat before they reached Wake Island?

_____

4. What could happen during that time? _____

5. While Tony worried about the sea, what was Rosa doing? _____

Part 2

Write the words.

1. wade   + ing = _____
2. figure   + ed = _____
3. sparkle + er = _____
4. drag   + ing = _____
5. drench + ed = _____
6. carry   + ing = _____

7. remove + ed = _____
8. hard   + ly = _____
9. wonder + ed = _____
10. muffle + ed = _____
11. measure + ing = _____
12. heave   + ed = _____

Details, suffixes

Name _____

On the Sea

The sun was setting and the bugs were beginning to come	11
out when Rosa, Tony, and Salt pushed the boat away from the	23
shore. All agreed that it would be better to start back that night	36
than to wait until morning. If they waited until morning, they	47
would have to sleep up on the mountain, far from the boat. If	60
they tried to sleep near the boat, they wouldn't get much sleep,	72
with the bugs hounding them all night. So they agreed that it	84
was best to start their trip back that night.	93
"Rrr-rrr-rrr," went the starter. "Chu-cug, chu-cug," went	100
the engine. Salt was right. The boat was riding low in the water.	113
Even though Salt had left most of the tools in the jungle, the	126
weight of the gold in the front of the boat was pushing the nose	140
down.	141
Salt, Tony, and Rosa were near the back of the boat. Rosa	153
put her arm over the side and measured the distance from the	165
top of the boat to the water. It was only about a foot. A	179
good-sized wave would wash right into the boat.	187
But the sea was very calm and the stars were reflected in the	200
water.	201

A Note to the Parent

Listen to the student read the passage. Count the number of words read in one minute and the number of errors.

Number of words read _____ Number of errors _____

We read the story _____ times.

(Parent's/Listener's) signature _____

Date _____

Reading fluency

Name _____

Part 1 Read the words in the box. Then fill in the blanks.

darkness	squinted	place	tense	slowly	appeared
far	hard	planned	quickly	poured	stars
compass	figured	time	calm	reflected	worried
tiller	pointed	steered	supposed	bucket	decided

Morning was near now. This was the _____ they were _____

to reach Wake Island. Salt's face was _____. His head moved

_____—looking this way and that way.

"We should be seeing lights any time," Salt said. But no lights _____. Salt

looked up at the _____. Then he checked his compass. Then he began to look

this way and that way again.

"I think I see something," Rosa said from the front of the boat. "Over there." She

_____ to the west.

Tony _____ and looked where Rosa was pointing. He looked as

_____ as his eyes could look, but he didn't see anything.

Part 2 Write the two words that make up each compound word.

1. herself   =   _____   +   _____

2. motorcycle   =   _____   +   _____

3. throughout   =   _____   +   _____

4. outside   =   _____   +   _____

5. somewhere   =   _____   +   _____

6. anyone   =   _____   +   _____

Part 3 Write the words.

1. was + not = _____   3. we + will = _____

2. what + is = _____   4. I + have = _____

Vocabulary/context, compound words, contractions

Name _____

Part 4

Never Make Light of the Sea

Salt was in the front of the boat. He had just picked up	13
a bag of gold and had told Tony that he was going to do	27
something to save the boat. Salt threw a sack of gold. But he	40
didn't throw it into the ocean. He threw it to the middle of the	54
boat. Then he threw another bag, and another, and another.	64
After he had moved more than ten of the bags, he came back to	78
the tiller.	80
He hollered, "This will put more weight in the back of the	92
boat. The front will be higher in the water. Maybe the waves	104
won't come over it now."	109
Tony was still bailing. It didn't seem to be doing much to get	122
rid of the water in the bottom of the boat. For every bucketful	135
removed from the boat, a wave added a bucketful. It went on	147
that way for about an hour.	153
The back of the boat was only a little bit above the water.	166
Every now and then it would sink below the surface of the	178
water for a moment, and water would pour in over the back.	190
Every now and then a huge wave would break against the front	202
of the boat and send water flying into the boat.	212

A Note to the Parent

Listen to the student read the passage. Count the number of words read in one minute and the number of errors.

Number of words read _____ Number of errors _____

We read the story _____ times.

(Parent's/Listener's) signature _____

Date _____

Reading fluency

Lesson 60

Name _____

Part 1

Write the words without endings.

1. scrambled   _____
2. grinning   _____
3. nearly   _____
4. imagined   _____
5. touching   _____

6. tiller   _____
7. supposed   _____
8. driving   _____
9. tangled   _____
10. clapped   _____

Part 2

Write the words.

1. had   +   not   = _____
2. she   +   will   = _____
3. he   +   is   = _____
4. would   +   not   = _____
5. I   +   had   = _____

6. they   +   had   = _____
7. do   +   not   = _____
8. you   +   have   = _____
9. I   +   will   = _____
10. will   +   not   = _____

Part 3

1. Write the work **knock.** Circle **kn.** _____

2. Write the word **surface.** Make a line under **ce.** _____

3. Write the word **invitation.** Make a line under **tion.** _____

4. Write the word **huge.** Circle **ge.** _____

Suffixes, contractions, copying words

Part 4

The Long Night

The engine had died. Tony and the others were somewhere	10
in the South Pacific Ocean. They were more than a hundred	21
miles from Wake Island. The sea was still rough. The boat was	33
turning sideways and rocking as the waves struck it from the	44
side.	45
"What's wrong?" Tony asked.	49
"I won't know until I look at the engine." Salt removed the	61
metal cover from the engine. The engine looked small and old.	72
Salt bent over it. He grabbed the spark plug. "Hit the starter,"	84
he said to Rosa.	88
"Rrr-rrr-rrr."	89
"That's enough," Salt said. "The engine is not getting a	99
spark. Something's wrong with the ignition system."	106
Salt took out his knife and touched different parts of the	117
engine. Then he shook his head. "The magneto is wet," he said.	129
"What do we do now?" Tony asked.	136
"Wait," Salt said. "The sun is bright and hot. With the cover	148
off the engine, it should dry out in a little while."	159
Salt tried the starter every fifteen minutes. The third time he	170
tried it, the engine started.	175
"Good deal," Tony yelled. "We're on our way again."	184
"Yes we are," Salt said, but he shook his head.	194
"What's wrong?" Tony asked.	198
"We drifted quite a bit while the engine was dead," Salt said.	210

A Note to the Parent

Listen to the student read the passage. Count the number of words read in one minute and the number of errors.

Number of words read _____ Number of errors _____

We read the story _____ times.

(Parent's/Listener's) signature _____

Date _____

Reading fluency

Name _____

Part 1

Read the sentences in the box and answer the questions.

> Rosa said, "Do you think Tony and I should give some of our gold away?"
>
> "No," Salt barked. "That gold is yours. You keep it and make good use of it. Just don't let it change your life. Remember, the gold is not the real treasure. The real treasure is the treasure hunt. The treasure is doing things and having good friends with you."
>
> Tony remembered what Salt said. He remembered it for years, and he tried to follow the advice that Salt had given him. Tony didn't buy a lot of motorcycles and cars. He didn't act as if he were a big-timer. He and Rosa helped their mother and father buy a new house. Tony went back to school, and he worked hard. After he graduated, he went on to college and worked hard. Whenever he got a chance, he went to visit Old Salt.

1. According to Salt, what is the real treasure? _____

_____

2. Name four things Tony did that show he tried to follow Salt's advice. _____

_____

_____

_____

Part 2

Write the two words that make up each word.

1. motorboat = _____ + _____

2. afternoon = _____ + _____

3. loudspeaker = _____ + _____

4. sunset   = _____ + _____

5. airport   = _____ + _____

6. forever   = _____ + _____

7. throughout = _____ + _____

8. sideways   = _____ + _____

Part 3

Write the two words that make up each word.

1. can't = _____ + _____

2. here's = _____ + _____

3. didn't = _____ + _____

4. that's = _____ + _____

5. you're = _____ + _____

6. wasn't = _____ + _____

Story theme, compound words, contractions

Name _____

Part 4

The Trip Home

Tony and the others slept in the truck. When Tony woke up,	12
the truck was moving. Salt was driving the truck and singing,	23
" 'Tis a sailor's life for me, for me. For I sail the seven seas—"	37
"Where are we going now?" Rosa asked.	44
"To the airport, Rosa, to the airport."	51
Salt parked in front of the airport in a no-parking zone.	62
Then he got out of the truck.	69
"If a cop comes over here," Salt said, "tell him I'll punch	81
him in the nose if he tries to give us a ticket."	93
"Do you really want us to tell him that?" Rosa asked.	104
"I sure do," Salt said. "Tell it like you mean it. I'll feel a lot	119
better with a cop standing next to this truck."	128
Salt went into the airport. Just then a police car pulled up	140
next to the truck.	144
"Move that truck," the cop said.	150
"We can't," Tony said. "We don't have the keys. But the man	162
who is driving this truck said that he'd punch you in the nose if	176
you gave us a ticket."	181
"He said that, did he?" the cop said. He got out of his car	195
and walked to the front of the truck.	203

A Note to the Parent

Listen to the student read the passage. Count the number of words read in one minute and the number of errors.

Number of words read _____   Number of errors _____

We read the story _____ times.

(Parent's/Listener's) signature _____

Date _____

Reading fluency

Lesson 62

Name _____

Part 1

Write **1, 2, 3,** or **4** in front of each sentence to show when these things happened in the story. Then write the sentences in the blanks.

_____ Rosa parked the car in the driveway in front of the old sailors' home.

_____ Somebody snapped on the lights, and everybody yelled, "Surprise."

_____ Old Salt loaded his fishing gear into the car, and the car took off down the street.

_____ Tony, Rosa, and Salt went up the front steps and inside the building.

1. _____

_____

2. _____

_____

3. _____

_____

4. _____

_____

Part 2

Write the words.

1. report + er = _____

2. wheeze + ed = _____

3. quiet + ly = _____

4. arrive + ed = _____

5. range + er = _____

6. office + er = _____

7. figure + ing = _____

8. disappear + ed = _____

9. graduate + ed = _____

10. move + ing = _____

11. plan + ed = _____

12. bang + ed = _____

Part 3

1. Write the word **howled.** Make a line over the **ow.** _____

2. Write the word **reformed.** Underline **or.** _____

Sequence, suffixes, copying words

Part 4

Salt's Real Treasure

The day after Salt and the others came home, Tony was	11
reading accounts of the treasure hunt in the newspaper. One	21
account said that they came back with sixteen bags of gold.	32
"That's not right," Tony said.	37
He glanced through another account. It said the same thing.	47
It said that Salt and Tony and Rosa had found twenty-four	58
sacks but brought back only sixteen.	64
The account said, "When Salt was asked what happened to	74
the other sacks, he said, 'They went back to the sea.' "	85
Tony tossed the newspaper aside. He got Rosa and they ran	96
from the house. They ran all the way to Salt's house. Salt was	109
sitting on the front steps talking to three people.	118
Tony said, "Salt, can we go inside? We want to ask you	130
something."	131
"Sure," Salt said.	134
So Tony, Rosa, and Salt went inside. They went upstairs to	145
Salt's room. It seemed to Tony that it was a hundred years ago	158
when they had been in that room before, looking at the map,	170
trying to figure out how to crack the code.	179
Tony asked, "How many bags did we bring back?"	188
"I can see it in your face," Salt said. "You're thinking that	200
Old Salt stole some of your gold."	207

A Note to the Parent

Listen to the student read the passage. Count the number of words read in one minute and the number of errors.

Number of words read _____ Number of errors _____

We read the story _____ times.

(Parent's/Listener's) signature _____

Date _____

Reading fluency

Name _____

Part 1 Write the name of the person each sentence tells about.

Emma Branch   president   Rosa   Old Salt   con man

1. This person passed out the ostrich eggs.   _____

2. This person said, "Come on, Salt. We can beat these bums."   _____

3. This person said, "Take one big step back. Throw your eggs."   _____

4. This person did not throw the egg far enough, and Tony dropped it._____

5. This person said, "Our next event will be a pie-eating contest."_____

6. This person was the first to get a pie in the face.   _____

7. This person tossed a pie and hit the rancher right in the face.   _____

8. This person grabbed the con man by the back of the neck and
   pushed his face into a pie.   _____

Part 2 Write the words.

1. invite   +   ed   =   _____   6. remember + ed   =   _____

2. mad   +   er   =   _____   7. snap   + ed   =   _____

3. blame   +   ed   =   _____   8. live   + ly   =   _____

4. argue   +   ing =   _____   9. quick   + ly   =   _____

5. ranch   +   er   =   _____   10. wave   + ed   =   _____

Part 3 Write the words.

1. we   +   will   = _____   3. does +   not   = _____

2. is   +   not   = _____   4. I   +   will   = _____

Characterization, suffixes, contractions

Part 4

A Surprise Party

It was Salt's birthday, so Rosa and Tony decided to throw	11
a big party at the old sailors' home. Rosa and Tony wanted to	24
surprise Salt, so they didn't tell him about the party. But they	36
tried to invite all of the people that he had talked about.	48
He had once talked about a rancher named Emma Branch,	58
so they invited her. One time Salt had told a tale about a funny	72
con man, so they invited him. And of course they invited all of	85
the old people who lived in the home—men and women who	97
had spent their lives sailing and fishing.	104
On the day of the party, Rosa and Tony went over to Salt's	117
home. They pulled up in Rosa's car. "Salt," they called, "let's go	129
for a little outing."	133
Salt said, "I'm ready for an outing. I thought I would go	145
down to the stream and see if I could catch some trout."	157
"We wanted to go for a drive," Rosa said. "But why don't	169
you bring your fishing gear along? We may find a place to do	182
some fishing."	184
So Old Salt loaded his gear into the car, and the car took	197
off down the street.	201

A Note to the Parent

Listen to the student read the passage. Count the number of words read in one minute and the number of errors.

Number of words read _____   Number of errors _____

We read the story _____ times.

(Parent's/Listener's) signature _____

Date _____

Reading fluency

Name _____

Part 1

Write the name of the person each sentence tells about.

Stan	president	Thin Jim	Fuzz	con man

1. This person got out of the water and again explained the rules

   of the pie-eating contest. _____

2. This person brought out another load of pies. _____

3. This person won the pie-eating contest. _____

4. This person always wears three pairs of socks. _____

5. This person won a gold toothpick. _____

6. This person said, "I can't help it if I got jungle sickness." _____

7. This person said, "Our next event will be the sale." _____

8. This person put a baseball mitt on his foot. _____

9. This person dragged out a box that was almost as big as he was. _____

Part 2

Write these words without endings.

1. hollered _____
2. sticky _____
3. laughing _____
4. finished _____
5. flying _____
6. cheered _____
7. rancher _____
8. received _____

9. matches _____
10. battling _____
11. folks _____
12. yelling _____
13. glasses _____
14. leading _____
15. dragged _____
16. having _____

Characterization, suffixes

Part 3

The Egg-Throwing Contest

Salt, Rosa, the rancher, and everybody else ran outside. Salt	10
and Emma Branch were partners. Rosa and Tony were partners.	20
All of the old sailors paired off. Some of them were laughing	32
and horsing around.	35
"Silence," the president said. "We must have silence."	43
Everybody became quiet and looked at the president. Next	52
to him was a huge basket.	58
"To make the game more interesting, we have large eggs," the	69
president said.	71
Salt said, "Those are ostrich eggs. They are bigger than	81
baseballs."	82
The con man passed out the eggs. The old folks laughed and	94
talked with each other.	98
"Silence," the president said. "Everybody, line up and begin	107
the game. Throw your eggs."	112
There were about thirty pairs of people playing the game.	122
The eggs went into the air. Everybody caught the eggs except	133
one man named Stan. His egg landed on his shirt with a "splat."	146
Everybody but that man and his partner laughed.	154
Stan, the man who missed the egg, was madder than	164
someone covered with cotton-taffy pike. He said to his partner,	174
"Pete, you didn't have to throw a line drive at me."	185
"Line drive, my foot," Pete said. "If you had put your	196
glasses on, you might have caught that egg."	204

A Note to the Parent

Listen to the student read the passage. Count the number of words read in one minute and the number of errors.

Number of words read _____ Number of errors _____

We read the story _____ times.

(Parent's/Listener's) signature _____

Date _____

Reading fluency

Lesson 65

Name _____

Part 1
Write the words.

1. shake + ing = _____
2. grin + ing = _____
3. smile + ed = _____
4. quiet + ly = _____
5. figure + ing = _____
6. quick + er = _____

7. yell + ed = _____
8. eat + en = _____
9. drip + ed = _____
10. glance + ed = _____
11. slight + ly = _____
12. smart + est = _____

Part 2
Write the two words that make up each compound word.

1. newspaper = _____ + _____
2. upstairs = _____ + _____
3. myself = _____ + _____
4. driveway = _____ + _____
5. birthday = _____ + _____
6. underline = _____ + _____

7. backpack = _____ + _____
8. everyone = _____ + _____
9. inside = _____ + _____
10. toothpick = _____ + _____
11. watermelon = _____ + _____
12. sunshine = _____ + _____

Part 3
Write the words.

1. were + not = _____
2. where + is = _____
3. they + are = _____
4. I + am = _____

5. we + have = _____
6. could + not = _____
7. here + is = _____
8. you + will = _____

Suffixes, compound words, contractions

Name _____

Part 4

The Sale

Salt was having a surprise party. Pies were flying, people	10
were being tossed into the water, and everybody was getting	20
sore sides from laughing so hard.	26
The old people had tossed the president into the water.	36
"Please," the president said, "we must have a little order."	46
The president went back to the table and again explained	56
the rules of the pie-eating contest. The con man brought out	67
another load of pies, and the contest began.	75
"Glub, glump, chump, chump." Everybody ate pie and more	84
pie. Pretty soon a very fat man said, "That's all. I'm finished. I	97
hate pie." Everybody laughed.	101
The president spotted one person feeding pie to a dog under	112
the table. A woman was trying to feed her pie to an ostrich, but	126
the ostrich didn't like the pie. The ostrich liked a button on the	139
woman's coat.	141
"Get out of here, you giant turkey," the woman yelled.	151
The winner of the pie-eating contest was a tall, slim man	162
named Thin Jim. After everybody else quit, Thin Jim was still	173
putting pie away. "I'm just getting down to my all-day pace. I	185
could eat like this for days. I can eat more than anyone in these	199
parts. I can eat more than—"	205

A Note to the Parent

Listen to the student read the passage. Count the number of words read in one minute and the number of errors.

Number of words read _____ Number of errors _____

We read the story _____ times.

(Parent's/Listener's) signature _____

Date _____

Reading fluency

Answer Key

Part 1
Write these words without endings.

1. stripes   _stripe_
2. stinker   _stink_
3. noses   _nose_
4. smaller   _small_

5. choked   _choke_
6. blushed   _blush_
7. closer   _close_
8. talked   _talk_

Part 2
Read the words in the box. Then fill in the blanks.

horse	ten	garden	six	tips	striped
see	five	mad	stripes	smell	stand
stinker	brown	hear	proud	middle	look

There were _five_ stink bugs that lived in a _garden_. Stink bugs are proud if they can make a big stink. The biggest stink bug was very _proud_. She said, "This is how to make a stink." And she made a big stink that you could _smell_ on the other side of the garden.

One stink bug had a _striped_ back. He said, "If a bug has stripes on its back, it has the best _stinker_. Here I go."

Part 3
Copy the sentences.

A bird was flying over the garden.
A bird was flying over the garden.

The smallest bug had stripes on its back.
The smallest bug had stripes on its back.

We are in the middle of a contest.
We are in the middle of a contest.

Name _____

Part 4
Write these words with ed endings.

1. jump   _jumped_
2. fish   _fished_
3. form   _formed_

4. talk   _talked_
5. smell   _smelled_
6. trick   _tricked_

Part 5
Read the sentences in the box. Then write the answer to each question.

> The little bug kept talking. She said, "One time, I made a stink that was so powerful it turned all the grass brown. I'll bet that I can beat ten skunks in a stinking contest."

1. What happened when the little bug made a powerful stink? _The grass turned brown._

2. What did the little bug bet? _(She bet that she could beat ten skunks in a stinking contest.)_

Part 6
Match the words and complete them.

snow   _____ chomping

chomping   _____ sings

sings   _____ summer

night   _____ snow

summer   _____ night

A Note to the Parent

Work was completed at home.

_____ _____
(Parent's/Listener's) signature   Date

Lesson 2

Name _____

Part 1
Write these words without endings.

1. talking   talk
2. taking   take
3. striped   stripe
4. bigger   big

5. shopped   shop
6. stinker   stink
7. closed   close
8. packed   pack

Part 2
Match the words and complete them.

forest   st**and**

began   si**ck**

stand   **glad**

sick   **for**est

glad   be**gan**

Part 3
Read the sentences in the box. Then write the answer to each question.

The little bug asked, "Are you grabbing on to something? Nobody can stand up when my stink reaches them. First it hits them so hard that they fall down. Then it knocks the air from them. And when it has done that, my stink chokes them up. But most bugs don't die from the smell. They are just sick for weeks."

1. What is the first thing that happens to other bugs when they smell the little bug's stink?

They fall down.

2. How long are the bugs sick from the stink?   for weeks

Lesson 2

Name _____

Part 4
Read the words in the box. Then fill in the blanks.

trying	fort	cloud	best	telling	leave
fainting	contest	smallest	stand	shown	told
left	blush	garden	whiff	taking	stinking

There was a contest in the garden . Five stink bugs were trying to see who had the best stinker. All of the bugs but one had shown off their best stink. Now that bug began telling the others how good she was at stinking . She talked and talked. The other bugs began to leave . Soon only the biggest bug was left .

Part 5
Write these words with er endings.

1. cold   colder   5. deep   deeper
2. stick   sticker   6. fast   faster
3. hard   harder   7. help   helper
4. talk   talker   8. stink   stinker

Part 6
Copy the sentences.

Breathe in deeply and hold in the air.

Breathe in deeply and hold in the air.

She went to the other side of the garden.

She went to the other side of the garden.

A Note to the Parent   Work was completed at home.

_____ (Parent's/Listener's signature)   _____ Date

Name _____

Part 1

Write these words without endings.

1. asked ___ ask ___
2. loner ___ lone ___
3. winked ___ wink ___
4. skipped ___ skip ___

5. making ___ make ___
6. planned ___ plan ___
7. walked ___ walk ___
8. closer ___ close ___

Part 2

Follow the instructions for each item.

1. Write the word couch. Make a line under ou. ___ couch ___
2. Write the word coach. Make a line over oa. ___ coach ___
3. Write the word pail. Make a line over ai. ___ pail ___

Part 3

Write these words with er endings.

1. tell ___ teller ___
2. farm ___ farmer ___
3. teach ___ teacher ___
4. old ___ older ___

Part 4

Write these words with ing endings.

1. wait ___ waiting ___
2. laugh ___ laughing ___
3. look ___ looking ___
4. walk ___ walking ___

Suffixes, sound/symbol correspondence

Lesson 3   5

Name _____

Part 5

Match the words and complete them.

pond — _thir_ teen
grow — _grow_
thirteen — _pond_
block — _tried_
tried — _bl_ ock

Part 6

Read the sentences in the box. Then write the answer to each question.

After school, Art didn't hang out with the other kids in his class. He went home to work on the farm. The other kids in his class said, "Art's a loner. He never hangs out with us." They didn't know that Art was shy.

1. What did Art do after school? _He went home to work on the farm._

2. Why did the other kids say, "Art is a loner"? _(because he never hangs out with the other kids)_

Part 7

Copy the sentences.

He skipped stones on the pond. _He skipped stones on the pond._

She went to class on time. _She went to class on time._

Word completion, inferences, copying sentences

6   Lesson 3

Lesson 4

Name _____

Part 1
Write these words with ed endings.

1. coach _coached_

2. blush _blushed_

3. toss _tossed_

Part 2
Write these words with es endings.

1. coach _coaches_

2. blush _blushes_

3. toss _tosses_

Part 3
Write the two words that make up each word.

1. herself = _her_ + _self_

2. basketball = _basket_ + _ball_

3. sometimes = _some_ + _times_

4. motorboat = _motor_ + _boat_

5. everyone = _every_ + _one_

6. anything = _any_ + _thing_

Part 4
Write these words without endings.

1. raising _raise_

2. grabbed _grab_

3. smiled _smile_

4. nearly _near_

5. sailed _sail_

6. deeply _deep_

7. skipping _skip_

8. roses _rose_

Vocabulary/suffixes, compound words

Lesson 4   7

Lesson 4

Name _____

Part 5

Lonely Art

Art was a farm boy. He talked like a farm boy. He walked   13
like a farm boy. And when he was thirteen years old, he began   26
to grow. When he was fifteen years old, he was taller than any   39
other kid. His arms seemed too long. He looked like a long   51
blade of grass.   54

After school, he didn't hang out with the other kids in his   66
class. He went home to work on the farm. The other kids in his   80
class said, "Art's a loner. He never hangs out with us." They   92
didn't know that Art was shy.   98

A teacher in the school told Art that he should go out   110
for basketball. And Art did. But he hadn't played basketball   120
before. And he wasn't any good. He couldn't shoot the ball. He   132
couldn't block shots. He couldn't dribble the ball.   140

The coach said, "Art, this game is too hard for you. Why   152
don't you try out for another sport?"   159

But Art didn't try another sport. After school, he went   169
down to the pond near his farm house. He skipped stones on   181
the pond. He said to himself, "I just wish there were a   193
stone-skipping team. I'd be the champ of that team."   202

A Note to the Parent

Listen to the student read the passage. Count the number of words read in one minute and the number of errors.

Number of words read _____ #   Number of errors _____ #

We read the story _____ # times.

(Parent's/Listener's signature _____ _Signature_

Date _____ _Date_

Reading fluency

8   *Lesson 4*

Lesson 5

Name _____

Part 1
Write these words with **er** endings.

1. play   player
2. small   smaller
3. catch   catcher
4. long   longer

Part 2
Write these words with **ed** endings.

1. lean   leaned
2. walk   walked
3. yell   yelled
4. dress   dressed

Part 3
Write the two words that make up each word.

1. baseball = base + ball
2. someone = some + one

Part 4
Write **1**, **2**, or **3** in front of each sentence to show when these things happened in the story. Then write the sentences in the blanks.

  3   Art didn't sleep well that night.

  1   Art tossed pitches to the catcher.

  2   The coach said, "Art, I would like you to come out for baseball."

1. Art tossed pitches to the catcher.

2. The coach said, "Art, I would like you to come out for baseball."

3. Art didn't sleep well that night.

Suffixes, compound words, sequence

Lesson 6

Name _____

Part 1
Write these words without endings.

1. whipped   whip
2. laughing   laugh
3. leaned   lean
4. tallest   tall
5. raises   raise
6. blushed   blush
7. stones   stone
8. faking   fake

Part 2
Match the words and complete them.

started   deeply

springing   smiled

deeply   started

smiled   springing

closer   closer

Part 3
Write **1**, **2**, or **3** in front of each sentence to show when these things happened in the story. Then write the sentences in the blanks.

  2   Art kept telling himself what he should not do.

  1   Art didn't sleep well before the game with West High.

  3   He leaned back and tossed the ball about nine feet over the catcher's mitt.

1. Art didn't sleep well before the game with West High.

2. Art kept telling himself what he should not do.

3. He leaned back and tossed the ball about nine feet over the catcher's mitt.

Suffixes, word completion, sequence

138

Lesson 7

Name _____

Part 1
Read the sentences and answer the questions.

Art remembered that Bob was the best batter on the West team.
For a moment, Art began to think about the things that he should not do.

1. Who was Bob? _the best batter on the West team_ (the

2. When Art remembered about Bob, what did Art begin to think about? _(the
   things that he should not do)_

3. For how long did Art think about those things? _(a moment)_

Part 2
Write these words without endings.

1. deeply _____ deep
2. grabbed _____ grab
3. loudly _____ loud
4. smartest _____ smart
5. baker _____ bake
6. taking _____ take
7. smiling _____ smile
8. muttered _____ mutter

Part 3
Read the words in the box. Then fill in the blanks.

stared	start	up	hugged	sat	passed
hit	leaned	cheered	pitch	swing	shake
jumped	throw	down	reached	clapped	tossed

Art _leaned_ back and—"Zip—pow." The catcher was _down_. And the
batter began to _swing_ after the ball had _reached_ the catcher.

The fans from Art's school cheered and cheered. They _jumped_ up and down. They
hugged each other. They yelled, "Go to it, Art. Show them how to pitch."

Details, suffixes, vocabulary/context clues

Copyright © SRA/McGraw-Hill. Permission is granted to reproduce for classroom use.

Lesson 7   13

Lesson 8

Name _____

Part 1
Read the sentences in the box. Then write the answer to each question.

After the first game, things were different in school. The kids smiled at Art. They went
out of their way to talk to him. Art felt a lot better about school. In fact, school was a lot
of fun for Art now. He waved to the girls. He wasn't afraid to talk to girls. He didn't look
down when he talked to them. He had done that before, but now he was Art the Star, the
big pitcher.

1. When were things different in school for Art? _(after the first game)_

2. Name two ways that things were different in school. _(the kids smiled at
   Art; he wasn't afraid to talk to girls)_

3. Why wasn't Art afraid to talk to the girls now? _because he was Art
   the Star, the big pitcher_

Part 2
Write these words without endings.

1. rider _____ ride
2. riding _____ ride
3. smiles _____ smile
4. remembered _____ remember
5. groaned _____ groan
6. patted _____ pat

Part 3
Read the sentences and answer the questions.

Art said to Patty, "If that's the way you want it," and walked down the hall.
He started to whistle, just to show her that he didn't care if she went with him.

1. Who walked down the hall? _Art_

2. Why did Art start whistling? _(because he wanted to show Patty
   that he didn't care if she went with him)_

3. What did Art do as he walked down the hall? _(whistled)_

Make inferences, suffixes, draw conclusions based on evidence

Copyright © SRA/McGraw-Hill. Permission is granted to reproduce for classroom use.

Lesson 8   15

Name _____

Part 1
Follow the instructions for each item.

1. Write the word **would**. Make a line over **oul**. $\overline{would}$

2. Write the word **almost**. Make a line over **al**. $\overline{al}most$

3. Write the word **ducked**. Make a line under **ck**. $duc\underline{ked}$

Part 2
Write these words with ed endings.

1. play   played
2. whistle   whistled
3. jog   jogged

Part 3
Write these words with er endings.

1. bat   batter
2. start   starter
3. play   player

Part 4
Read the sentences in the box. Then write the answer to each question.

> Before the game, some fans didn't cheer. One of the fans said, "We didn't come here to see kids play. We came to see the Reds and the Tigers."
> Art walked to the mound. Then he looked up at the stands. He had never seen so many fans before. Suddenly he became afraid. He began to think about all of the things that he shouldn't do. "Don't throw the ball too high," he told himself.

1. Why didn't some fans cheer? (because they came to see professional ball players, not kids)

2. When Art looked up at the stands, what did he see? (He saw more fans than he had ever seen before.)

3. What did Art say to himself? Don't throw the ball too high.

Sound/symbol correspondence, suffixes, details

Name _____

Part 1
Read the sentences in the box. Then write the answer to each question.

> People from the big league came over to talk to Art that night. A man from the Reds said that he would pay Art three hundred thousand dollars if Art left school and became a pitcher for the Reds. A woman from the Tigers told Art that she would give Art five hundred thousand dollars if Art played with the Tigers.
> Art told them that he would have to think about leaving school.
> Then some of Art's friends came over. They wanted to take Art to a party. Art asked his dad and mom, and they said that it was all right for him to go.

1. How much money were the Tigers offering to give to Art if he came and pitched for them? five hundred thousand dollars

2. Why did Art want to take time to think about the offers from the two baseball teams? (He wanted to decide if he should leave school.)

3. Who told Art it was okay to go to the party? (His parents said it was okay.)

Part 2
Write the name of the person or the people each sentence tells about.

Art	Art's mom and dad	Art's friends
Woman from the Tigers	Art's friends	Man from the Reds

1. These people asked Art to go to a party with them. Art's friends
2. This person offered Art $300,000 to play baseball. Man from the Reds
3. This person asked to go to a party. Art
4. This person offered Art $500,000 to play baseball. Woman from the Tigers
5. These people said Art could go to a party. Art's mom and dad

Draw conclusions based on evidence, skim and scan for information/character identification

140

Name _____

Part 1
Read the sentences in the box. Then write the answer to each question.

Art didn't talk to Patty for a month. He moped around the farm. He went to the doctor's office three times a week. The doctor had him do exercises for his arm.

Now Art could bend his arm almost all the way. But his arm was weak. It was so weak that he couldn't bend it when he held a heavy steel ball. The doctor told him that he sho 'id exercise his arm at home every day, but Art didn't feel like exercising. So his arm didn't get very strong.

1. Art moped around school and around the farm. What does **mope** mean? _(act sad and depressed)_

2. What did the doctor tell Art that he should do? _exercise his arm at home every day_

3. Why didn't Art's arm get very strong? _(because Art was not exercising it)_

Part 2
Write these words with ed endings.

1. sail _____ sailed
2. clap _____ clapped
3. lean _____ leaned
4. pass _____ passed
5. scratch _____ scratched

Part 3
Write these words with ing endings.

1. yell _____ yelling
2. think _____ thinking
3. sit _____ sitting
4. dream _____ dreaming
5. drive _____ driving

Draw conclusions based on evidence, suffixes

Name _____

Part 1
Write these words without endings.

1. nearly _____ near
2. speaker _____ speak
3. leaving _____ leave
4. winner _____ win
5. falling _____ fall
6. mixed _____ mix
7. skipped _____ skip
8. smallest _____ small

Part 2
Match the words and complete them.

itched _____ con**t**est

flying _____ f**ea**red

contest _____ fl**y**ing

noses _____ itch**ed**

feared _____ no**s**es

Part 3
Write the two words that make up each word.

1. handshake = hand + shake
2. basketball = basket + ball
3. somewhere = some + where
4. spotlight = spot + light

Suffixes, compound words, word completion

Lesson 14

Part 1
Read the sentences in the box. Then write the answer to each question.

> Now Art was afraid. A player was on third base. There was one out. And Art didn't have a flashing fast ball that would strike out the other batters.
> The catcher jogged out and said to Art, "Just make the old brain work, Art. You can strike this next guy out. Just throw the kind of pitch he's not looking for. Watch me. I'll give you some signals."
> So Art watched the catcher. The catcher signaled for a slow curve. "No," Art said to himself. "He'll hit it out of the park." Then Art began to think, "Maybe he won't. Maybe he's looking for a very fast ball. Maybe a curve will throw his timing off and make him miss the ball."

1. Art didn't have his flashing fast ball. What is a **flashing** fast ball?
(a pitch that moves very fast)

2. What did the catcher tell Art? (He told Art to make his brain work; to throw a pitch that the batter didn't expect; to watch him for some signals)

3. What kind of pitch did the catcher signal for? a slow curve

4. Why could that kind of pitch trick the batter? (It could throw off the batter's timing.)

Part 2
Write the words. Items 1 and 3 are done for you.

1. I	+	will	=	I'll
2. he	+	will	=	he'll
3. did	+	not	=	didn't
4. would	+	not	=	wouldn't
5. is	+	not	=	isn't

Conclusions, contractions

Lesson 14 27

Lesson 13

Part 1
Write the words.

out	+	side	=	outside
any	+	where	=	anywhere
your	+	self	=	yourself
cheer	+	leader	=	cheerleader

Part 2
Read the sentences in the box. Then write the answer to each question.

> Art said, "I once read that a bird with a broken wing never flies as high again."
> Patty said, "Stop that. You're not a bird, and you don't have a broken wing. They fixed your arm. You just have to start being brave."
> Art glared at her. "What do you mean? What makes you think I'm not brave?"

1. What did Art say about a bird with a broken wing? A bird with a broken wing never flies as high again.

2. Art thinks that he is a bird with a broken wing. What does he mean by that? (He thinks that he'll never be good at baseball again.)

3. What did Patty tell Art that he should do? Start being brave.

4. Art glared at Patty. What does **glare** mean? (to stare angrily at someone)

Part 3
Write these words without endings.

1. watched	watch	5. skipped	skip
2. nodded	nod	6. feeling	feel
3. taken	take	7. broken	broke
4. making	make	8. harder	hard

Making deductions, suffixes, compound words

Lesson 13 25

142

Name _____

Part 1

Write these words with er endings.

1. speak   _speaker_
2. pitch   _pitcher_
3. fast   _faster_
4. bat   _batter_

Part 2

Write these words with ing endings.

1. talk   _talking_
2. start   _starting_
3. stop   _stopping_
4. think   _thinking_

Part 3

Read the sentences in the box. Then write the answer to each question.

The president was standing next to the cab. He said to the con man, "Get out of that cab this instant."

The con man got out of the cab. He was thinking to himself, "I must find a way to get away from this guy."

The president said, "Before we leave on our trip, we must find some fine duds. Who would think of going on a trip without fine duds?"

1. The president told the con man to get out of the cab this instant. What does this instant mean? _(right now, at this moment)_

2. What does the con man want to do? _(He wants to get away from the president.)_

3. What are fine duds? _(nice clothes)_

(Note: Accept reasonable spelling of "clothes.")

Part 4

Write these words without endings.

1. driver   _drive_
2. faking   _fake_
3. taken   _take_
4. escaped   _escape_
5. smiled   _smile_
6. grabbed   _grab_

Suffixes, conclusions

Name _____

Part 1

Write the words. Item 1 is done for you.

1. he + is = _he's_
2. there + is = _there's_
3. you + will = _you'll_
4. I + will = _I'll_
5. did + not = _didn't_
6. has + not = _hasn't_

Part 2

Read the words in the box. Then fill in the blanks.

started	mistake	watched	list
pitched	picked	stormed	fuss
guys	shocked	stared	bags
strokes	lies	dashed	tried
			past
			mess
			expected
			desk

The president looked _shocked_. He _stared_ at the list of names.

Then he said, "I am sorry for making such a _fuss_. I was so upset about our _bags_ that I must have looked right _past_ the name on the list."

The president was telling _lies_ left and right. He had just _picked_ the name Henry Reeves from the _list_ and had given it to the con man.

Part 3

Write these words with ly endings.

1. proud   _proudly_
2. slow   _slowly_
3. clean   _cleanly_

Part 4

Write these words with ing endings.

1. wait   _waiting_
2. ship   _shipping_
3. catch   _catching_

Contractions, vocabulary/context clues, suffixes

Lesson 18

Name _____

Part 1
Read the passage and answer the questions.

A tall man had found out that the con man was trying to steal his bags. The con man was trying to think of something to say, but the words were not flowing from his mouth. He was stammering and stuttering and saying, "You know—I mean, you see. . . ." The tall man was getting very mad.

Then suddenly the president came back. He had a cop with him. He said, "There he is, officer. That tall man is the impostor. Go ask him his name, and you'll see."

The cop went up to the tall man. "All right, buddy," he said. "What's your name?" "Fredrick. Robert Fredrick," the tall man said. "And this man seems to be stealing my bags."

1. What did the president tell the cop? (He told the cop that the tall man was the impostor.)

2. What did the tall man say his name was? Robert Fredrick

3. What did the tall man say was going on? (He said that the con man was trying to steal his bags.)

Part 2
Write these words without endings.

1. rubbed	rub	5. piped	pipe
2. nosed	nose	6. lonely	lone
3. opening	open	7. shouted	shout
4. quickly	quick	8. flowing	flow

Details, suffixes

Lesson 18   35

Lesson 17

Name _____

Part 1
Write the words.

1. with + out = without
2. over + sight = oversight
3. every + body = everybody
4. some + where = somewhere

Part 2
Read the sentences in the box. Then write the answer to each question.

As the woman called the shipping department, the president turned to the con man and whispered, "I don't want to tell them that I am a president. That would scare them. So I'll just pretend that I'm another person."

The steamship woman said, "I'm happy to report that all of your bags are safe in our shipping department."

The president turned to the con man and said, "You fool. You told me that our bags were not in the shipping department. You must try to take more care when I give you a task to do."

The con man didn't say a thing. He just looked at the president. The con man said to himself, "If I am a con man, the president is a super con man."

1. What did the woman say about the bags? (She said that the bags were safe in the shipping department.)

2. What did the president do next? (He called the con man a fool; he told the con man to take more care with his jobs.)

3. What did the con man think of the president? (He thought the president was a super con man.)

Part 3
Write these words without endings.

1. hopped	hop	4. turned	turn
2. hopes	hope	5. missing	miss
3. taken	take	6. hardly	hard

Compound words, details, suffixes

Lesson 17   33

Lesson 19

Name _____

Part 1
Follow the instructions for each exercise.

1. Write the word **partner**. Make a line over ar.   p̄artner

2. Write the word **person**. Make a line over er.   p̄erson

3. Write the word **loaded**. Make a line under oa.   lōaded

Part 2
Read the words in the box. Then fill in the blanks.

crying	slept	homesick	stammer	plan
spent	hollow	open	start	hollered
demand	crouch	smiling	guy	care
buddy	escape	different	stared	conned

"I have ___spent___ three years at Happy Hollow," the president said. He was

still ___smiling___. "Those were the best three years of my life. When the cop said,

'Happy Hollow,' I became ___homesick___."

The con man was thinking that he would have to ___start___ all over. He

would have to ___plan___ some way to get out of the rest home. He said to

himself, "The next time I ___escape___, I won't be ___conned___ into going

with a ___guy___ like the president."

Part 3
Write the words. Item 1 is done for you.

1. they + had = they'd
2. I + had = I'd
3. you + had = you'd
4. I + will = I'll
5. could + not = couldn't
6. here + is = here's

Sound/symbol correspondence, vocabulary/context clues, contractions

Lesson 19   37

Lesson 20

Name _____

Part 1
Write the two words that make up each word.

everything	=	every	+	thing
homesick	=	home	+	sick
understand	=	under	+	stand
without	=	with	+	out

Part 2
Read the sentences in the box. Then write the answer to each question.

> Hurn tried to back away from the big cat. But he felt the hard rock of the cave against his back. He could go back no more. Surt was curled next to him.
> Without knowing why he did it, Hurn showed his teeth and began to growl. He snapped at the air as if to scare the cat away. The cat stopped for an instant, but then it started to come toward the puppies again.

1. Why couldn't Hurn back away from the big cat? (There was no room to move in the cave.)

2. Name three things Hurn did to try to scare the cat away. (showed his teeth, began to growl, snapped at the air)

3. What did the cat do next? (It stopped for an instant, and then it moved closer.)

Part 3
Write these words without endings.

1. smelling   smell
2. smiles   smile
3. closer   close
4. flashing   flash
5. snapped   snap
6. noses   nose
7. catcher   catch
8. cheering   cheer

Compound words, details, suffixes

Lesson 20   39

Name _____

Part 1
Write the words.

1. sudden	+	ly	=	suddenly
2. howl	+	ed	=	howled
3. long	+	er	=	longer
4. time	+	s	=	times
5. reach	+	es	=	reaches

Part 2
Read the words in the box. Then fill in the blanks.

curled	toward	fell	staring
fire	dash	care	ferns
roasting	rustling	rising	reached
chunk	turning	jumped	hurry

stepped	
crouched	
burned	
might	

Suddenly there was a __rustling__ sound in the __ferns__ next to Hurn. Hurn turned. The sound came from Surt. She was running __toward__ the spit. She was running as fast as her legs would take her. She __reached__ the spit before any of the men saw her, and she might have gotten away with a big __chunk__ of deer meat—except for one thing. She __stepped__ in the fire. She had never seen fire before. She had been in such a __hurry__ to get the meat that she didn't take as much __care__ as she should have.

Part 3
Write these words without endings.

1. tossed	toss	5. broken	broke
2. softly	soft	6. takes	take
3. shines	shine	7. hunter	hunt
4. following	follow	8. popped	pop

Suffixes, vocabulary/context clues

Name _____

Part 1
Write the words. Item 1 is done for you.

1. I	+	have	=	I've		
2. you	+	have	=	you've		
3. did	+	not	=	didn't		
4. there	+	is	=	there's		
5. you	+	will	=	you'll		
6. is	+	not	=	isn't		

Part 2
Read the sentences in the box. Then write the answer to each question.

> The pups stood in the cold water, shivering and scanning the air with their noses. Slowly the pups walked from the water. But they did not go back to the cave. Something told them that the cave was no longer safe. Something said to Hurn, "Stay away from the cave." So Hurn and Surt began to follow the bank of the stream. Hurn led the way. Surt followed. From time to time she tried to play with her brother, but Hurn wouldn't play.

1. When the pups stood in the water, what did they do with their noses?
(They scanned the air.)

2. Why didn't the pups go back to the cave? (Something told them that the cave was no longer safe.)

3. Where did the pups go after they got out of the stream? (along the bank of the stream)

4. Which wolf pup still wanted to play? Surt

Part 3
Match the words and complete them.

quickly		shivering
shivering		thirsty
reached		quickly
wheeze		reached
thirsty		wheeze

Contractions, details, word match

146

Lesson 23

Name _____

Part 1
Read the words in the box. Then fill fill in the blanks.

something	pat	water	walking	playing
sniffing	slowly	brother	fiddle	somewhere
smelling	friend	trumpet	three	poke
mother	limping	quickly	all	push

As the man played the ___fiddle___, Surt began to walk ___slowly___ down the hill toward the men. She was still ___limping___, but she walked on ___all___ of her paws. She walked over to Vern and sat down next to him. The men did not see her do this.

Surt sniffed the air. She was ___smelling___ the meat. She wanted some more meat, but she wanted ___something___ else, too. She missed her ___mother___. She wanted a friend. So she leaned over and gave Vern a little ___poke___ with her nose.

Part 2
Read the sentences in the box. Then write the answer to each question.

> One of the men was stirring the beans. Another was sitting near the spit. Vern sat on the other side of the fire. And Hurn was trying to hear everything and see everything. But he didn't move. The only things that moved were his sides as he breathed.

1. Who was stirring the beans? _(one of the men)_

2. Where was Vern? _(sitting on the other side of the fire)_

3. Hurn stayed very still. What part of him moved? _(His sides moved as he breathed.)_

4. Why do you think Hurn didn't move? _(He was hiding because he sensed danger.)_

Vocabulary/context clues, details

Lesson 24

Name _____

Part 1
Write these words without endings.

1. wagged	wag	5. howling	howl
2. softly	soft	6. followed	follow
3. stepping	step	7. watched	watch
4. piled	pile	8. sitting	sit

Part 2
Read the sentences in the box. Then write the answer to each question.

> Hurn wanted to curl up and sleep. He wanted to dream about eating or running or chasing butterflies. But when he was done with his drink, he began walking upstream along the bank of the stream.
>
> He felt like going back to the cave, but he didn't remember how to get to the cave. And he remembered that the cave was not his home any more. He had to find a new cave. He had to find a friend. So he walked and walked.

1. What did Hurn do after he had a drink at the stream? _(He began walking upstream along the bank of the stream.)_

2. Why didn't he go back to the cave? _(He didn't remember how to get there, and it was not his home any more.)_

3. Name two things Hurn needed to do. _(He had to find a new cave, and he had to find a new friend.)_

Part 3
Write the two words that make up each part.

1. didn't	=	did	+	not
2. I'll	=	I	+	will
3. here's	=	here	+	is

Suffixes, details, contractions

Lesson 26

Name _____

Part 1
Read the sentences in the box. Then write the answer to each question.

> Then the tan wolf began to walk up the slope, past the other wolves. When she was part way up the slope, she stopped and waited for Hurn. He ran up behind her and tried to hide under her. She held her head up and walked on past the other wolves. They stared at her as she passed.

1. How did the tan wolf show that she wanted Hurn to follow her? *(When she was part way up the slope, she stopped and waited for him.)*

2. Why did Hurn try to hide under her? *(He was afraid of the other wolves.)*

3. What did the other wolves do as the tan wolf walked past them? *They stared at her.*

Part 2
Write the two words that make up each word.

1. outside   =   _out_   +   _side_
2. daytime   =   _day_   +   _time_
3. campfire   =   _camp_   +   _fire_
4. someday   =   _some_   +   _day_
5. upwind   =   _up_   +   _wind_

Part 3
Write the two words that make up each word.

1. you'll   =   _you_   +   _will_
2. isn't   =   _is_   +   _not_
3. I've   =   _I_   +   _have_

Inferences, compound words, contractions

Lesson 26   51

Lesson 25

Name _____

Part 1
Write the words.

1. stiff + ly = _stiffly_
2. tug   + ed = _tugged_
3. whine + ed = _whined_
4. scan   + ing = _scanning_
5. miss   + ed = _missed_
6. stare + ing = _staring_

Part 2
Read the words in the box. Then fill in the blanks.

nipped	followed	closed	beat	yawned
ran	eat	sniffed	dashed	snuggled
harm	standing	opening	sneaked	tired
back	blinked	howled	stared	realized

Hurn _followed_ the tan wolf back to her den. There he met her pup. He was sleeping, curled up in a little ball. Hurn _sniffed_ at Hurn. When she felt that Hurn would not _harm_ her pup, she _yawned_. Then she turned around three times and lay down with her nose toward the _opening_ of the den.

Hurn _snuggled_ up next to her. They looked like two balls of fur. Hurn was so, so tired. He _blinked_ two times. Then his eyes closed, and he went to sleep.

Suffixes, vocabulary/context clues

Lesson 25   49

148

Lesson 27 and Lesson 28 worksheets

Lesson 27

Name _____

Part 1
Read the sentences in the box and answer the questions.

> The fox was very smart. It would bite off bits of fur and drop them on the bank of the stream. Then the fox would swim to the other side of the stream. The idea was to get the wolves mixed up.
>
> And the plan almost worked. The wolves came to the bank of the stream. They smelled the bits of fur. The smell was very strong. It was so strong that the wolves could smell nothing else. They ran around and around, but they always came back to the bits of fur.

1. What did the fox do to trick the wolves? It bit off bits of fur and dropped them on the bank of the stream.

2. Why did the bits of fur fool the wolves? (The fur smelled so strong that the wolves couldn't smell anything else.)

3. Where was the fox? It was on the other side of the stream.

Part 2
Write the words.

1. smart + er = smarter
2. roll + ed = rolled
3. jog + ed = jogged
4. gaze + ed = gazed
5. chase + ing = chasing
6. quick + ly = quickly

Part 3
Write the words.

1. could + not = couldn't
2. you + had = you'd
3. there + is = there's

Details, suffixes, contractions

Lesson 28

Name _____

Part 1
Read the words in the box. Then fill in the blanks.

hill	best	piled	summer	trick	plants	winner
black	fall	boss	tan	animals	ground	easy
hard	winter	mountain	fish	drifts	bite	backed
fight	brown	stacks	swirled			

Hurn didn't have to fight any of the other wolves. They seemed to know that Hurn was boss. Maybe they knew from the way he had gone at the black wolf.

Late in the fall, Hurn led the other wolves to high ground, way up the side of a mountain. They would spend the winter up there, and they would not have an easy time. The trees were not tall, and there were not many animals.

The snow came early. It swirled down every night. Before the middle of December, the snow had piled up in drifts that were twenty feet high.

Part 2
Write the two words that make up each word.

1. hasn't = has + not
2. I'll = I + will
3. you've = you + have
4. wouldn't = would + not

Part 3
Write the words.

1. loud + est = loudest
2. get + ing = getting
3. fool + ed = fooled
4. puzzle + ed = puzzled
5. near + ly = nearly

Vocabulary/context clues, contractions, suffixes

Lesson 30

Name _____

Part 1
Match the words and complete them.

inventor — base**ment**
experiment — **fac**tory
basement — experi**ment**
complain — in**vent**or
factory — com**plain**

Part 2

1. Write the word **lousy**. Make a line over the **ou**.   l͞ousy
2. Write the word **point**. Make a line under the **oi**.   p͟oi͟nt
3. Write the word **boarding**. Make a line over the **oa**.   b͞oarding
4. Write the word **toil**. Make a line under the **oi**.   t͟oi͟l
5. Write the word **folded**. Make a line under the **ol**.   f͟ol͟ded

Part 3
Write the words.

1. like + ed = liked
2. bright + ly = brightly
3. invent + or = inventor
4. board + ing = boarding
5. starve + ed = starved

Part 4
Write the words.

1. some + body = somebody
2. may + be = maybe
3. with + out = without
4. every + one = everyone
5. an + other = another

Word match, word parts, suffixes, compound words

Lesson 29

Name _____

Part 1
Write these words without endings.

1. slowly — slow
2. crouched — crouch
3. rubbed — rub
4. bothered — bother
5. starved — starve
6. friendly — friend
7. piles — pile
8. chasing — chase

Part 2
Read the sentences in the box. Then write the answer to each question.

Hurn didn't walk away from the wolf pup. Hurn got above the wolf pup and grabbed her by the nape of the neck. He gave a hard jerk. The pup let out a yelp, but now the pup was free. The pup wagged her tail and rolled over on her back to show Hurn that she was boss and that she would do what she wanted her to do.

1. What did Hurn do to the wolf pup? (He grabbed her by the nape of the neck, gave a hard jerk, and freed her.)

2. The pup let out a yelp. What is a yelp? (a cry or bark)

3. Why did the pup roll over on her back? to show Hurn that he was the boss

Part 3
Write the words.

1. he + is = he's
2. is + not = isn't
3. you + have = you've
4. here + is = here's

Suffixes, details, contractions

Lesson 31

Name _____

Part 1
Match the words and complete them.

recall   pret **zel**
hammer   re **call**
crazy   **foolish**
pretzel   ham **mer**
foolish   **crazy**

Part 2
Write the words.

1. listen + ed = __listened__
2. stick + y = __sticky__
3. drop + ing = __dropping__
4. flat + er = __flatter__
5. walk + ing = __walking__
6. dent + s = __dents__

Part 3
Write the two words that make up each word.

1. yourself = __your__ + __self__
2. downstairs = __down__ + __stairs__
3. anything = __any__ + __thing__
4. paintbrush = __paint__ + __brush__
5. anyone = __any__ + __one__

Word match, suffixes, compound words

Lesson 32

Name _____

Part 1
Write the words. Item 1 is done for you.

1. do + not = __don't__
2. you + will = __you'll__
3. she + is = __she's__
4. would + not = __wouldn't__
5. I + had = __I'd__
6. we + have = __we've__

Part 2
Write the words without endings.

1. watching __watch__
2. wadded __wad__
3. chores __chore__
4. beaches __beach__
5. smiled __smile__
6. dropped __drop__
7. relatives __relative__
8. stinky __stink__

Part 3
Write the words.

1. up + stairs = __upstairs__
2. some + thing = __something__
3. any + body = __anybody__
4. how + ever = __however__
5. with + out = __without__
6. day + light = __daylight__

Contractions, suffixes, compound words

Part 1

Write the name of the person each sentence tells about.

Herman   Carl   Irma   Berta   Fern

1. This person said, "I don't know why we stay here. She is all for herself. She never thinks about anybody else."

Berta

2. This person said, "Here is the hand you wanted," and held up her right hand.

Irma

3. This person looked at the hand. His lips moved, but his voice did not seem to be working.

Herman

4. This person looked at the hand and said, "Uh, buh, duh, buh, uh."

Carl

Part 2

Fill in the circle next to the word that completes the sentence. Write the word in the blank.

1. Herman sat on the _couch_ and watched TV.   ○ coach ● couch

2. Irma dumped the _paint_ from the jar.   ● paint ○ point

3. In a _loud_ voice, she said, "You wanted me to give you a hand?"   ○ lead ● loud

4. Fern stopped talking and _stared_ at the hand.   ○ starred ● stared

Part 3

Write the words.

1. wave + ed = _waved_   4. joke + s = _jokes_

2. bake + ing = _baking_   5. stop + ed = _stopped_

3. face + ing = _facing_   6. stare + ed = _stared_

Part 1

Write these words without endings.

1. stopped _stop_   5. glasses _glass_

2. hoped _hope_   6. tossed _toss_

3. waking _wake_   7. grabbed _grab_

4. staring _stare_   8. making _make_

Part 2

Write the words. Item 1 is done for you.

1. does + not = _doesn't_   4. he + is = _he's_

2. do + not = _don't_   5. they + had = _they'd_

3. we + will = _we'll_   6. I + have = _I've_

Part 3

Fill in the circle next to the word that completes the sentence. Write the word in the blank.

1. Berta ran from the room as fast as a track _star_ .   ○ stare ● star

2. Irma _rubbed_ the rag on the invisible paint.   ● rubbed ○ robbed

3. Fern was just _waking_ up again.   ○ walking ● waking

Name _____

Part 1
Write the words. Items 1, 5, and 9 are done for you.

1. I + am = I'm
2. I + will = I'll
3. he + will = he'll
4. she + is = she's
5. he + has = he's
6. it + is = it's
7. do + not = don't
8. does + not = doesn't
9. we + are = we're
10. you + are = you're

Part 2
Write these words without endings.

1. flipped — flip
2. closed — close
3. drapes — drape
4. places — place
5. offering — offer
6. really — real
7. remarked — remark
8. smiled — smile

Part 3
Write the two words that make up each word.

1. inside = in + side
2. herself = her + self
3. something = some + thing

Contractions, suffixes, compound words

152

Name _____

Part 1
Read the words in the box. Then fill in the blanks.

grab	meal	scare	fast	anything	chore
mean	right	listen	main	something	now
bold	yell	stand	stare	remember	careful
quiet	next	remarked	note	tone	stand

Irma said, "I have __something__ to say, and I am going to say it right now. And I want you to __listen__."

"All right, all right," Carl said. "Say what you have to say. Just make it __fast__."

Irma said, "From now on, don't __yell__ at me. Don't tell me to do every __chore__ around this house. And don't be __mean__ to me."

Berta said, "Who do you think you are, talking to me in that __tone__ of voice?"

"You know very well who I am," Irma said. "Just __remember__ what I'm telling you."

"Oh, be __quiet__, and let's eat," Carl __remarked__.

Part 2
Write the words.

1. eat + en = eaten
2. bother + ing = bothering
3. boil + ed = boiled
4. complain + ing = complaining
5. taco + s = tacos
6. daze + ed = dazed
7. scare + ed = scared
8. mix + ed = mixed

Vocabulary/context clues, suffixes

Part 1

Write the name of the person each sentence tells about.

Irma	Berta	Fern	Herman	Carl

1. This person said, "Who has my keys? Give them back right now." **Carl**

2. This person said, "Will you cut the noise? I can't even hear what they're saying on TV." **Fern**

3. This person was yelling, "I want my keys." **Carl**

4. This person was yelling, "I hope you can find them, so that you can get out of here, you bum." **Berta**

5. This person was yelling, "I don't know anything about your lousy keys." **Herman**

6. This person was laughing. **Irma**

Part 2

Write the words. Items 1 and 3 are done for you.

1. what + is = **what's**
2. that + is = **that's**
3. can + not = **can't**
4. I + am = **I'm**
5. do + not = **don't**

6. was + not = **wasn't**
7. we + are = **we're**
8. were + not = **weren't**
9. she + has = **she's**
10. you + have = **you've**

Characterization, contractions

Part 1

Read the sentences in the box and answer the questions.

> Irma had done some things to start an argument between her boarders. She had removed Carl's keys from his coat and slipped them into Herman's pocket. She had taken a glass and placed it next to Carl. Then she had taken a chunk of ice from the glass and dropped it down Berta's back.
>
> Now everybody was yelling. Carl was yelling because he couldn't find his keys. Berta was yelling because of the ice down her back. Fern was yelling because the others were making so much noise that she couldn't watch TV. And Herman was yelling because Carl was yelling at him about the keys.

1. Why was Carl yelling? He couldn't find his keys.

2. Where had Irma put the keys? She put them into Herman's pocket.

3. Why was Berta yelling? She had a chunk of ice down her back.

4. What'd Fern want to do? She wanted to watch TV.

5. Why was Herman yelling? Because Carl was yelling at him about the keys.

Part 2

Write these words without endings.

1. opened   **open**
2. removed   **remove**
3. placed   **place**
4. wearing   **wear**

5. pizzas   **pizza**
6. worker   **work**
7. hardly   **hard**
8. slipped   **slip**

Details, suffixes

Lesson 39

Name _____

Part 1
Write the words.

1. what + is = what's
2. you + are = you're
3. should + not = shouldn't
4. that + is = that's
5. we + will = we'll
6. does + not = doesn't
7. we + have = we've
8. I + am = I'm
9. can + not = can't
10. you + had = you'd

Part 2
Fill in the circle next to the word that completes the sentence. Write the word in the blank.

1. Irma will lend him money to pay the dentist's bill. ○ land ● lend
2. It was a bother for her to get the paint off. ● bother ○ brother
3. She fumbled around on the work bench until she found the invisible glasses. ● bench ○ beach
4. She left the room and waited to see what would happen. ○ wanted ● waited

Part 3
Write the compound words.

1. every + one = everyone
2. some + times = sometimes
3. in + side = inside
4. down + stairs = downstairs
5. it + self = itself
6. through + out = throughout

Contractions, vocabulary/context clues, compound words

Lesson 40

Name _____

Part 1
Read the words in the box. Then fill in the blanks.

simmering	nice	brother	tacos	fish	smiled
arguing	stared	smiles	complain	spilled	slipped
tired	bother	cheese	yelled	pizza	cola
peace	started	complaining	late	scared	warned

Now Irma's boarders didn't **bother** her. They didn't yell. They didn't **complain**. They seemed to be tired of **arguing**. In fact, Herman was even **nice** to her from time to time. One time she came home with a **late** **pizza**. Carl **started** to say something about how late she was, and Herman said, "Listen here. She works in that **cheese** factory all day and still brings us dinner. So stop **complaining**." Irma **smiled** at Herman and said, "Well, thank you, Herman. That was a very nice thing for you to say."

Part 2
Write the words without endings.

1. fumbles — fumble
2. simmering — simmer
3. slipped — slip
4. prices — price
5. smiled — smile
6. scared — scare
7. whistled — whistle
8. nearly — near

Vocabulary/context clues, suffixes

Lesson 41

Name _____

Part 1

Fill in the circle next to the word that completes the sentence. Write the word in the blank.

1. Then one day, Irma made up her __mind__ to keep the paint. ● mind ○ mine

2. From time to time, Berta would start to __gripe__ about Irma. ○ grip ● gripe

3. When this happened, Herman would say, "Stop __griping__." ○ gripping ● griping

4. It's so nice and __quiet__ in this room. ● quiet ○ quite

Part 2
Write the two words that make up each word.

1. downstairs = __down__ + __stairs__
2. yourself = __your__ + __self__
3. billboard = __bill__ + __board__
4. everybody = __every__ + __body__
5. outside = __out__ + __side__
6. nothing = __no__ + __thing__
7. anyone = __any__ + __one__
8. bedroom = __bed__ + __room__

Part 3
Write the words.

1. was + not = __wasn't__   3. I + have = __I've__
2. there + is = __there's__   4. should + not = __shouldn't__

Vocabulary/context, compound words, contractions

Copyright © SRA/McGraw-Hill. Permission is granted to reproduce for classroom use.

Lesson 41   81

Lesson 42

Name _____

Part 1
Read the sentences in the box and answer the questions.

When Old Salt had first moved into that little white house a year before, the girls and boys hadn't made fun of him. They listened to Old Salt tell about his days as a first officer on cargo ships. They heard him tell about the First World War and the Second World War. They listened to his tales about a chest of gold that had been taken from the SS *Foil* just before it had gone down in the South Pacific. The old man told the boys and girls that the *Foil* had sunk in 1918, while World War I was going on.

1. For how long had Old Salt lived in the house? __one year__

2. What job did he have on cargo ships? __first officer__

3. What did he say was taken from the SS *Foil* before it sank? __a chest of gold__

4. What is the South Pacific? __an ocean__

5. What was going on in the year 1918? __World War I__

Part 2
Write these words without endings.

1. retired __retire__   6. later __late__
2. relatives __relative__   7. loved __love__
3. mumbled __mumble__   8. liking __like__
4. really __real__   9. certainly __certain__
5. worker __work__   10. tales __tale__

Part 3
Write the words.

1. he + would = __he'd__   3. they + are = __they're__
2. what + is = __what's__   4. had + not = __hadn't__

Details, suffixes, contractions

Copyright © S 4/McGraw-Hill. Permission is granted to reproduce for classroom use.

Lesson 42   83

155

Lesson 43

Name _____

Part 1

Write the words. Item 1 is done for you.

1. like + ing = liking
2. nose + ing = nosing
3. take + en = taken
4. try + ing = trying
5. decide + ed = decided
6. snap + ed = snapped
7. young + er = younger
8. store + ed = stored
9. magnify + ing = magnifying
10. kid + ing = kidding

Part 2

Write the two words that make up each compound word.

1. outside = out + side
2. everybody = every + body
3. matchbox = match + box
4. sometime = some + time
5. without = with + out
6. downstairs = down + stairs
7. herself = her + self
8. classroom = class + room

Part 3

Write the words. Item 1 is done for you.

1. will + not = won't
2. do + not = don't
3. she + is = she's
4. were + not = weren't
5. you + have = you've
6. we + will = we'll

156

Lesson 44

Name _____

Part 1

Read the words in the box. Then fill in the blanks.

unfold	thousand	hundreds	parted	specks	shipped
shaped	painted	dotted	decide	sense	crack
fumbled	meal	start	maps	numbers	spoil
spell	pointed	chance	knock	close	find

Old Salt said, "If only we could __find__ out where this island is, we would be off to a good __start__. But there must be a __thousand__ little islands in the South Pacific. This could be any one of them. Look for yourself."

Salt __pointed__ to a big wall map of the South Pacific. It was __dotted__ with li: le islands. Most of them looked like __specks__. You couldn't tell from the map if they were __shaped__ like an S, like a C, or like an I. All of them looked like little dots.

Salt said, "I think those __numbers__ at the top of the map tell where the island is. But I haven't been able to __crack__ the code."

Part 2

Write the words.

1. was + not = wasn't
2. will + not = won't
3. here + is = here's
4. that + is = that's
5. does + not = doesn't
6. we + are = we're

Part 3

1. Write the word **decide**. Make a line over **ci**. __decide__
2. Write the word **farther**. Make a line over **ar**. __farther__
3. Write the word **loudly**. Make a line under **ou**. __loudly__

Lesson 45

Name _____

Part 1
Match the words and complete them.

volcano   poi**son**
poison   **trea**sure
sprang   **thorns**
treasure   **vol**cano
thorns   **sp**rang

peace
speck
thousands
bunch
numbers

numbers
bunch
peace
speck
thousands

Part 2
Write the words.

1. make + ing = _making_
2. store + ed = _stored_
3. solve + ed = _solved_
4. hike + ing = _hiking_
5. pace + s = _paces_
6. peer + ed = _peered_
7. set + ing = _setting_
8. pass + ed = _passed_
9. large + er = _larger_
10. grip + ed = _gripped_

Part 3
Write the two words that make up each word.

1. won't = _will_ + _not_
2. where's = _where_ + _is_
3. couldn't = _could_ + _not_
4. I've = _I_ + _have_
5. you're = _you_ + _are_
6. she'll = _she_ + _will_

Word match, suffixes, contractions

Lesson 46

Name _____

Part 1
Read the sentences in the box and answer the questions.

> "How much is the gold worth?" Tony asked.
> "That's not a thing to be talking about," Salt said sharply. He looked boiling mad.
> "Don't talk about gold," he said.
> "I'm sorry, Salt," Tony said. "Are you going to see about getting a ship?"
> Salt shook his head, "Don't talk about that," he said. "Just go off to school and think about something else."
> So Tony went to school. It seemed like a long day. It seemed as if the three o'clock bell would never ring. But at last it did, and Tony ran all the way to Salt's house. Now he would find out about the ship.

1. What two things did Old Salt tell Tony not to talk about? _gold and the ship_

2. What did Salt tell Tony to do instead? _go to school and think about something else_

3. Why did the school day seem so long to Tony? _(he wanted to go to Salt's house; he wanted to find out about the ship)_

4. What did Tony hope to find out about after school? _the ship_

Part 2
Write these words without endings.

1. tales   _tale_
2. slowly   _slow_
3. getting   _get_
4. having   _have_
5. talked   _talk_
6. boiling   _boil_
7. stopped   _stop_
8. quickly   _quick_
9. places   _place_
10. sharper   _sharp_

Details, suffixes

Lesson 47

Name _____

Part 1
Read the sentences in the box and answer the questions.

> Rosa and Tony bent over the table. Salt talked very softly. He told them that a vacation ship was leaving for the South Pacific in three weeks. Salt said that he could get a job on that ship. The ship would go as far as Wake Island. From that point, Salt would have to rent a small boat and travel 300 miles to Rose Island.

1. What kind of ship was leaving for the South Pacific? __a vacation ship__

2. When would the ship leave? __in three weeks__

3. How did Salt plan to pay for the trip? __He would get a job on that ship.__

4. Where is Wake Island? __in the South Pacific__

5. How did Salt plan to get from Wake Island to Rose Island? __He would rent a small boat.__

6. How far is it from Wake Island to Rose Island? __300 miles__

Part 2
Write the words.

1. trap + ed = __trapped__
2. puddle + s = __puddles__
3. let + ing = __letting__
4. broke + en = __broken__
5. bite + ing = __biting__
6. sharp + ly = __sharply__

Part 3
Write the two words that make up each word.

1. won't = __will__ + __not__
2. there's = __there__ + __is__
3. you'll = __you__ + __will__
4. I'm = __I__ + __am__
5. they're = __they__ + __are__
6. can't = __can__ + __not__

Details, suffixes, contractions

Lesson 48

Name _____

Part 1
Read the words in the box. Then fill in the blanks.

placed	four	worked	kidding	week	grime
weak	stopped	fished	mess	cook	button
three	sailor	blazing	pointed	crime	painted
passed	boiler	streaked	showed	rammed	chunks

For __four__ hours Tony __fished__ clinkers from the furnace. He had a long, __pointed__ rod. He __rammed__ the rod into the clinkers. Then he lifted them from the furnace.

After four hours had __passed__, a __sailor__ came to Tony and said, "Okay, you're off for four hours." Tony was a __mess__. He was covered with grit and __grime__. His face was __streaked__ with sweat. His hands were sore. His legs were __weak__.

Part 2
Write the words.

1. late + er = __later__
2. change + ed = __changed__
3. pat + ed = __patted__
4. pile + ing = __piling__
5. carry + ing = __carrying__
6. open + ed = __opened__
7. quick + ly = __quickly__
8. hire + ed = __hired__

Part 3
Write the words.

1. It + is = __It's__
2. he + would = __he'd__
3. we + have = __we've__
4. she + has = __she's__

Vocabulary/context, suffixes, contractions

Lesson 49

Name _____

Part 1
Read the sentences in the box and answer the questions.

> The ship had made five stops. This was the last one. It would stay at Wake Island for three days. Then it would go back home. But Tony, Rosa, and Salt would not be on it. They would be in a small boat on their way to Rose Island.
> That night Tony, Rosa, and Salt were standing on the dock again, talking to a woman who had small boats for rent. The night air was sweet with the smell of wild flowers. And the air was hot and wet.
> Salt was saying to the woman at the dock. "We need a boat that can go six hundred miles out to sea."

1. For how long would the vacation ship stay at Wake Island? __three days__

2. When the ship went back home, where would Salt, Rosa, and Tony be? __in a small boat on their way to Rose island__

3. Why did they meet with the woman on the dock? __She had small boats for rent.__

4. What made the air smell sweet? __wild flowers__

5. How did the air feel? __The air felt hot and wet.__

6. What kind of boat did Salt say they needed? __one that can go six hundred miles out to sea__

7. How far is it from Wake Island to Rose Island? __300 miles__

Part 2
Write the words.

1. gripe + ing = __griping__
2. hard + ly = __hardly__
3. believe + ed = __believed__
4. wave + ing = __waving__
5. small + er = __smaller__
6. large + er = __larger__
7. move + ed = __moved__
8. slap + ing = __slapping__
9. final + ly = __finally__
10. like + ing = __liking__

Details, inferences, endings

Lesson 49   97

Lesson 50

Name _____

Part 1
Read the words in the box. Then fill in the blanks.

birds	place	pop	green	feet	string
beach	swim	distance	sheet	gallon	surface
wash	dock	melt	volcano	yellow	bring
shovels	ring	pile	bugs	wild	claws

The sky in the east was starting to turn __yellow__. The sea was as smooth as a __sheet__ of glass. Every now and then a little fish would __pop__ out of the water and leave a __ring__ that moved slowly and seemed to __melt__ into the smooth __surface__ of the water. The vacation ship was dark, except for the __string__ of lights on the top deck. Little birds were walking on the __beach__. So were big crabs with __claws__ that could cut off your finger. The __bugs__ seemed to be everywhere.

Part 2
Write the compound words.

1. every + where = __everywhere__
2. speed + boat = __speedboat__
3. flash + light = __flashlight__
4. out + fit = __outfit__
5. after + noon = __afternoon__
6. some + how = __somehow__
7. pass + port = __passport__
8. your + self = __yourself__
9. when + ever = __whenever__
10. any + thing = __anything__

Vocabulary/context, compound words

Lesson 50   99

Lesson 51

Name _____

Part 1
Read the sentences in the box and answer the questions.

The island didn't look the way Tony had thought it would. It looked much bigger than he had thought. And the cliffs were much higher than he had thought. At last the boat came to the place where there were no cliffs. There was a little cove. The water in the cove was clear and very green. Tony could see fish swimming under the surface of the water. The boat slid up on the black-sand beach. Salt cut the engine, and everything was calm, except for the hooting of birds.

1. Name two ways that the island looked different than Tony thought it would look.
(The island looked much bigger, and the cliffs were higher.)

2. Salt, Tony, and Rosa found a place to land the boat where there were no cliffs. What place was that? a little cove

3. What was the water like in the cove? clear and very green

4. What kind of beach did they land on? a black-sand beach

5. After Salt turned off the motor, what was the only sound they could hear?
the hooting of birds

Part 2
Write the words.

1. start	+ er	=	starter
2. slap	+ ed	=	slapped
3. snore	+ ed	=	snored
4. pile	+ ing	=	piling
5. spray	+ ed	=	sprayed
6. pace	+ ing	=	pacing
7. bounce	+ ed	=	bounced
8. shake	+ ing	=	shaking
9. speckle	+ ed	=	speckled
10. bob	+ ing	=	bobbing

Part 3
Write the words.

1. you	+ had	=	you'd
2. we	+ have	=	we've
3. do	+ not	=	don't
4. he	+ has	=	he's

Details/inferences, suffixes, contractions

Lesson 52

Name _____

Part 1
Read the words in the box. Then fill in the blanks.

stream	stopped	back	foot	dense	mapped
twisted	paced	top	letter	mopped	spray
arrow	left	filtered	edge	lucky	soaked
tied	slope	squinted	pointed	turned	ferns

They stopped at the edge of a stream. They jumped across the stream, turned more toward the west, and paced off another twenty-six paces. They stopped at the edge of the very steep slope.

"This must have been the foot of the volcano," Salt said. "So far we've been lucky. There has been a landmark for everything arrow on the map."

Now Salt and the others turned south. The map said W-16. So Salt stepped off twenty-three paces and stopped. There was no landmark.

Salt mopped the sweat from his face. He squinted and looked through the underbrush. "No landmark," he said. "But let's go on."

Part 2
Write the two words that make up each compound word.

1. underbrush	=	under	+ brush
2. landmarks	=	land	+ marks
3. sunlight	=	sun	+ light
4. southwest	=	south	+ west

Part 3
Write the words.

1. pace	+ ed	=	paced
2. slight	+ ly	=	slightly
3. rot	+ ing	=	rotting
4. holler	+ ed	=	hollered
5. excited	+ ed	=	excited
6. smile	+ ing	=	smiling

Vocabulary/context, compound words, suffixes

Lesson 54

Part 1 Read the words in the box. Then fill in the blanks.

knife	pushed	peered	rusty	bent	patted
find	bobbed	volcano	handle	paced	shovel
piles	traps	tugged	ledge	chain	bands
soil	scrambled	cove	corner	rocks	lock

Tony and Rosa _scrambled_ up the side of the _volcano_. Tony remembered to bring his _shovel_. When they reached the _ledge_, they saw Salt _bent_ over.

Without looking up, Salt said, "They put the treasure under the _knife_."

I don't see any more _traps_. Let's dig down and see what we _find_," Salt _pushed_ the shovel into the ground. "Clink." He tossed the dirt aside. And there it was, the _corner_ of the chest.

Part 2 Write the two words that make up each compound word.

1. breakfast = _break_ + _fast_
2. something = _some_ + _thing_
3. afternoon = _after_ + _noon_
4. nothing = _no_ + _thing_
5. maybe = _may_ + _be_
6. sunlight = _sun_ + _light_
7. landslide = _land_ + _slide_
8. whenever = _when_ + _ever_
9. daytime = _day_ + _time_

Part 3 Write the words.

1. here + is = _here's_
2. is + not = _isn't_
3. you + have = _you've_
4. were + not = _weren't_

Vocabulary/context, contractions, word parts

Lesson 54   107

Lesson 53

Part 1

Write 1, 2, 3, or 4 in front of each sentence to show when these things happened in the story. Then write the sentences in the blanks.

2 ___ Salt uncoiled a rope and tied one end of it around the handle of the knife.

1 ___ Tony found a knife handle in the pile of rocks.

4 ___ Suddenly, a huge pile of rocks came sliding down the side of the volcano.

3 ___ Salt tugged and tugged until the knife came out of the ground.

1. _Tony found a knife handle in the pile of rocks._

2. _Salt uncoiled a rope and tied one end of it around the handle of the knife._

3. _Salt tugged and tugged until the knife came out of the ground._

4. _Suddenly, a huge pile of rocks came sliding down the side of the volcano._

Part 2 Write the words.

1. he + had = _he'd_
2. it + is = _it's_
3. did + not = _didn't_
4. we + are = _we're_
5. where + is = _where's_
6. will + not = _won't_
7. you + will = _you'll_
8. I + am = _I'm_

Part 3 Write the words.

1. rumble + ing = _rumbling_
2. rust + y = _rusty_
3. rattle + ing = _rattling_
4. tug + ed = _tugged_
5. bite + ing = _biting_
6. cool + er = _cooler_

Sequence, contractions, suffixes

Lesson 53   105

Lesson 55

Name

Part 1
Read the sentences in the box and answer the questions.

The treasure didn't look the way Tony had thought that it would. He had thought that he would see heaps of shiny coins and gold crowns. He had thought that he would see huge red gems that sparkled and gold drinking cups. But he saw heaps of black coins. Some of them were covered with green mold. Some of them had specks of white on them, but most of them were black.

There were three or four bugs in the chest, too. They scrambled down between the coins when the chest was opened.

1. Name three things that Tony thought he would see in the treasure chest.
heaps of shiny coins, huge red gems, gold drinking cups

2. What did he see instead? heaps of black coins

3. What were some coins covered with? green mold

4. What happened to the bugs in the chest? They scrambled down between the coins.

Part 2
Write the words.

1. strange + er = stranger
2. have + ing = having
3. taste + ed = tasted
4. sudden + ly = suddenly
5. stop + ing = stopping

6. uncover + ed = uncovered
7. sparkle + ed = sparkled
8. dance + ing = dancing
9. mop + ed = mopped
10. stare + ing = staring

Part 3
Write the two words that make up each word.

1. shouldn't = should + not
2. that's = that + is
3. I'll = I + will
4. we've = we + have

Details, suffixes, contractions

Lesson 56

Name

Part 1
Write 1, 2, 3, or 4 in front of each sentence to show when these things happened in the story. Then write the sentences in the blanks.

2 Rosa, Tony, and Salt made eight trips to drag the sacks of gold down to the boat.

4 Salt said they would get the treasure home if the sea wanted them to take it home.

3 They figured out that 24 sacks of gold would be worth over seven million dollars.

1 Salt, Tony, and Rosa put pretty stones in the sacks to hide the gold.

1. Salt, Tony, and Rosa put pretty stones in the sacks to hide the gold.

2. Rosa, Tony, and Salt made eight trips to drag the sacks of gold down to the boat.

3. They figured out that 24 sacks of gold would be worth over seven million dollars.

4. Salt said they would get the treasure home if the sea wanted them to take it home.

Part 2
Read the paragraphs and answer the questions.

"Don't talk that way," Tony said. "We've got the gold, and we're going to get it home. Right, Rosa?"

"Right," Rosa said. "If we have to swim home with those sacks, we'll get them home. Right, Salt?"

Salt smiled. "Yes. We'll get it home if the sea wants us to take it home. And I hope that the sea does just that. But remember, our boat is going to ride low in the water. There will be nearly 2,000 pounds of weight in the front of the boat. A good squall could send our treasure to the bottom of the ocean. Let's just hope that the sea is calm and that no squalls come up."

1. What was in the front of the boat? (the gold; nearly 2,000 pounds of weight)

2. Why would the boat ride low in the water? because the gold was so heavy

3. What could happen if a squall came up? (A squall could cause the boat to sink, sending the treasure to the bottom of the ocean.)

Sequence, details/inferences

Lesson 57

Name _____

Part 1
Write **1**, **2**, **3**, or **4** in front of each sentence to show when these things happened in the story. Then write the sentences in the blanks.

4   The bottom of the boat had nearly a foot of water in it.

2   Within an hour, a stiff wind began to blow.

3   Before long, the waves were rolling and pounding into the side of the boat.

1   The air was foggy the next morning, and the sea was still very calm.

1. The air was foggy the next morning, and the sea was still very calm.

2. Within an hour, a stiff wind began to blow.

3. Before long, the waves were rolling and pounding into the side of the boat.

4. The bottom of the boat had nearly a foot of water in it.

Part 2
Read the words in the box. Then fill in the blanks.

side	hounding	boiling	rocking	stand	sink
sliding	size	lifting	sound	couple	bottom
setting	mass	limping	course	darker	foggy
gusts	foaming	floated	smell	head	scrambled

Before long, the waves were rolling and __boiling__ and pounding into the side of the boat. The fog was __lifting__ now, and Tony could see that the ocean was a __mass__ of white, __foaming__ waves. The boat was __rocking__ from side to side as the waves pounded against it. The __sound__ of the waves was very loud.

Salt said, "We're going to have to change __course__. Unless we __head__ into the wind, we'll __sink__. Those waves will soon be coming over the __side__ of the boat."

Sequence, vocabulary/context

Lesson 57   113

Lesson 58

Name _____

Part 1
Read the sentences in the box and answer the questions.

> Tony liked to think about the things that he could do with two million dollars. But every time he began to feel good about the gold, he remembered what Salt had said and became a little worried about the sea. Salt had said they wouldn't reach Wake Island until just before morning. They would still be in the boat all afternoon, all evening, and almost all of the night. That was a lot of time. And the sea could change quickly.
>
> Tony opened his eyes and looked around. Rosa was eating a banana. The sun was very hot.

1. What happened to Tony every time he began to feel good about the gold?
He remembered what Salt had said and became a little worried about the sea.

2. When would they reach Wake Island? just before morning

3. How much longer would they be in the boat before they reached Wake Island?
all afternoon, all evening, and almost all of the night

4. What could happen during that time? The sea could change quickly.

5. While Tony worried about the sea, what was Rosa doing? eating a banana

Part 2
Write the words.

1. wade + ing =   wading
2. figure + ed =   figured
3. sparkle + er =   sparkler
4. drag + ing =   dragging
5. drench + ed =   drenched
6. carry + ing =   carrying
7. remove + ed =   removed
8. hard + ly =   hardly
9. wonder + ed =   wondered
10. muffle + ed =   muffled
11. measure + ing =   measuring
12. heave + ed =   heaved

Details, suffixes

Lesson 58   115

Lesson 59

Name _____

Part 1 Read the words in the box. Then fill in the blanks.

darkness	squinted	place	tense	slowly	appeared
far	hard	planned	quickly	poured	stars
compass	figured	time	calm	reflected	worried
tiller	pointed	steered	supposed	bucket	decided

Morning was near now. This was the __time__ they were __supposed__ to reach Wake Island. Salt's face was __tense__. His head moved __quickly__—looking this way and that way.

"We should be seeing lights any time," Salt said. But no lights __appeared__. Salt looked up at the __stars__. Then he checked his compass. Then he began to look this way and that way again.

"I think I see something," Rosa said from the front of the boat. "Over there." She __pointed__ to the west.

Tony __squinted__ and looked where Rosa was pointing. He looked as __hard__ as his eyes could look, but he didn't see anything.

Part 2 Write the two words that make up each compound word.

1. herself = __her__ + __self__
2. motorcycle = __motor__ + __cycle__
3. throughout = __through__ + __out__
4. outside = __out__ + __side__
5. somewhere = __some__ + __where__
6. anyone = __any__ + __one__

Part 3 Write the words.

1. was + not = __wasn't__   3. we + will = __we'll__
2. what + is = __what's__   4. I + have = __I've__

Vocabulary/context, compound words, contractions

Lesson 60

Name _____

Part 1
Write the words without endings.

1. scrambled   __scramble__
2. grinning   __grin__
3. nearly   __near__
4. imagined   __imagine__
5. touching   __touch__
6. tiller   __till__
7. supposed   __suppose__
8. driving   __drive__
9. tangled   __tangle__
10. clapped   __clap__

Part 2
Write the words.

1. had + not = __hadn't__
2. she + will = __she'll__
3. he + is = __he's__
4. would + not = __wouldn't__
5. I + had = __I'd__
6. they + had = __they'd__
7. do + not = __don't__
8. you + have = __you've__
9. I + will = __I'll__
10. will + not = __won't__

Part 3

1. Write the work knock. Circle kn.   knock
2. Write the word surface. Make a line under ce.   surface
3. Write the word invitation. Make a line under tion.   invitation
4. Write the word huge. Circle ge.   huge

Suffixes, contractions, copying words

Lesson 61

Name _____

Part 1

Read the sentences in the box and answer the questions.

> Rosa said, "Do you think Tony and I should give some of our gold away?"
>
> "No," Salt barked. "That gold is yours. You keep it and make good use of it. Just don't let it change your life. Remember, the gold is not the real treasure. The real treasure is the treasure hunt. The treasure is doing things and having good friends with you."
>
> Tony remembered what Salt said. He remembered it for years, and he tried to follow the advice that Salt had given him. Tony didn't buy a lot of motorcycles and cars. He didn't act as if he were a big-timer. He and Rosa helped their mother and father buy a new house. Tony went back to school, and he worked hard. After he graduated, he went on to college and worked hard. Whenever he got a chance, he went to visit Old Salt.

1. According to Salt, what is the real treasure? __(the treasure hunt and__
__doing things with good friends)__

2. Name four things Tony did that show he tried to follow Salt's advice. __(He didn't__
__act like a big-timer. He and Rosa helped their parents__
__buy a new house. He went back to school. He visited Old__
__Salt when he got the chance.)__

Part 2

Write the two words that make up each word.

1. motorboat = __motor__ + __boat__   5. airport   = __air__ + __port__
2. afternoon = __after__ + __noon__   6. forever   = __for__ + __ever__
3. loudspeaker = __loud__ + __speaker__ 7. throughout = __through__ + __out__
4. sunset   = __sun__ + __set__   8. sideways = __side__ + __ways__

Part 3

Write the two words that make up each word.

1. can't = __can__ + __not__   4. that's = __that__ + __is__
2. here's = __here__ + __is__   5. you're = __you__ + __are__
3. didn't = __did__ + __not__   6. wasn't = __was__ + __not__

Story theme, compound words, contractions

Lesson 62

Name _____

Part 1

Write **1, 2, 3,** or **4** in front of each sentence to show when these things happened in the story. Then write the sentences in the blanks.

__2__ Rosa parked the car in the driveway in front of the old sailors' home.

__4__ Somebody snapped on the lights, and everybody yelled, "Surprise."

__1__ Old Salt loaded his fishing gear into the car, and the car took off down the street.

__3__ Tony, Rosa, and Salt went up the front steps and inside the building.

1. __Old Salt loaded his fishing gear into the car, and the__
__car took off down the street.__

2. __Rosa parked the car in the driveway in front of the__
__old sailors' home.__

3. __Tony, Rosa, and Salt went up the front steps and__
__inside the building.__

4. __Somebody snapped on the lights, and everybody__
__yelled, "Surprise."__

Part 2
Write the words.

1. report + er = __reporter__   7. figure + ing = __figuring__
2. wheeze + ed = __wheezed__   8. disappear + ed = __disappeared__
3. quiet   + ly = __quietly__   9. graduate + ed = __graduated__
4. arrive + ed = __arrived__   10. move   + ing = __moving__
5. range   + er = __ranger__   11. plan   + ed = __planned__
6. office + er = __officer__   12. bang   + ed = __banged__

Part 3

1. Write the word **howled**. Make a line over the **ow**. __howled__

2. Write the word **reformed**. Underline **or**. __reformed__

Sequence, suffixes, copying words

Lesson 63

Name _____

Part 1 Write the name of the person each sentence tells about.

Emma Branch   president   Rosa   Old Salt   con man

1. This person passed out the ostrich eggs. ___con man___

2. This person said, "Come on, Salt. We can beat these bums." ___Emma Branch___

3. This person said, "Take one big step back. Throw your eggs." ___president___

4. This person did not throw the egg far enough, and Tony dropped it. ___Rosa___

5. This person said, "Our next event will be a pie-eating contest." ___president___

6. This person was the first to get a pie in the face. ___con man___

7. This person tossed a pie and hit the rancher right in the face. ___Old Salt___

8. This person grabbed the con man by the back of the neck and pushed his face into a pie. ___president___

Part 2 Write the words.

1. invite + ed = ___invited___
2. mad + er = ___madder___
3. blame + ed = ___blamed___
4. argue + ing = ___arguing___
5. ranch + er = ___rancher___

6. remember + ed = ___remembered___
7. snap + ed = ___snapped___
8. live + ly = ___lively___
9. quick + ly = ___quickly___
10. wave + ed = ___waved___

Part 3 Write the words.

1. we + will = ___we'll___
2. is + not = ___isn't___
3. does + not = ___doesn't___
4. I + will = ___I'll___

Lesson 64

Name _____

Part 1
Write the name of the person each sentence tells about.

Stan   president   Thin Jim   Fuzz   con man

1. This person got out of the water and again explained the rules of the pie-eating contest. ___president___

2. This person brought out another load of pies. ___con man___

3. This person won the pie-eating contest. ___Thin Jim___

4. This person always wears three pairs of socks. ___Fuzz___

5. This person won a gold toothpick. ___Thin Jim___

6. This person said, "I can't help it if I got jungle sickness." ___Fuzz___

7. This person said, "Our next event will be the sale." ___president___

8. This person put a baseball mitt on his foot. ___Stan___

9. This person dragged out a box that was almost as big as he was. ___con man___

Part 2
Write these words without endings.

1. hollered ___holler___
2. sticky ___stick___
3. laughing ___laugh___
4. finished ___finish___
5. flying ___fly___
6. cheered ___cheer___
7. rancher ___ranch___
8. received ___receive___

9. matches ___match___
10. battling ___battle___
11. folks ___folk___
12. yelling ___yell___
13. glasses ___glass___
14. leading ___lead___
15. dragged ___drag___
16. having ___have___

Name _____

Part 1
Write the words.

1. shake + ing = _shaking_
2. grin + ing = _grinning_
3. smile + ed = _smiled_
4. quiet + ly = _quietly_
5. figure + ing = _figuring_
6. quick + er = _quicker_

7. yell + ed = _yelled_
8. eat + en = _eaten_
9. drip + ed = _dripped_
10. glance + ed = _glanced_
11. slight + ly = _slightly_
12. smart + est = _smartest_

Part 2
Write the two words that make up each compound word.

1. newspaper = _news_ + _paper_
2. upstairs = _up_ + _stairs_
3. myself = _my_ + _self_
4. driveway = _drive_ + _way_
5. birthday = _birth_ + _day_
6. underline = _under_ + _line_

7. backpack = _back_ + _pack_
8. everyone = _every_ + _one_
9. inside = _in_ + _side_
10. toothpick = _tooth_ + _pick_
11. watermelon = _water_ + _melon_
12. sunshine = _sun_ + _shine_

Part 3
Write the words.

1. were + not = _weren't_
2. where + is = _where's_
3. they + are = _they're_
4. I + am = _I'm_

5. we + have = _we've_
6. could + not = _couldn't_
7. here + is = _here's_
8. you + will = _you'll_

Suffixes, compound words, contractions

Lesson 65   **129**

167

Corrective Reading
Enrichment SRA Blackline Masters
Decoding B2 Decoding Strategies

Siegfried Engelmann

Gary Johnson

 SRA

Columbus, OH

SRAonline.com

 SRA

Send all inquiries to this address:
SRA/McGraw-Hill
4400 Easton Commons
Columbus, OH 43219

ISBN: 978-0-07-611234-0
MHID: 0-07-611234-9

   7 8 9 MAL 13 12 11 10

The *McGraw·Hill* Companies